The Internet
Job Search
Handbook

Andrea Semple
Matt Haig

How To Books

21.9.01

First published in 2001 by
How To Books Ltd, 3 Newtec Place,
Magdalen Road, Oxford OX4 1RE, United Kingdom
Tel: 01865 798306 Fax: 01865 248780

British Library Cataloguing in Publication Data
A catalogue record for this book is available from
the British Library

Edited by Peter Williams / Cover image PhotoDisc
Cover design by Shireen Nathoo Design

Produced for How To Books by Deer Park Productions
Typeset by PDQ Typesetting, Newcastle-under-Lyme, Staffs
Printed and bound in Great Britain by Bell & Bain Ltd.,
Glasgow

Note: The material contained in this book is set out in good
faith for general guidance and no liability can be accepted for
loss or expenses incurred as a result of relying in particular
circumstances on statements made in the book. The laws and
regulations are complex and liable to change, and readers
should check the current position with the relevant
authorities before making personal arrangements.

Contents

Preface

The Internet is rapidly becoming the ultimate job search tool. It is the world's largest careers library offering information on every type of job imaginable, and it also enables you to interact with people in similar jobs as well as to seek advice from employers themselves.

As more and more companies are discovering the benefits of online recruitment, so too are an ever growing number of job-hunters finding that the Internet is maximising their chances of securing a dream job.

While many people are now aware of the significance of the web and e-mail for job searching there remains a great deal of confusion regarding exactly when and how the Internet should be used for this purpose. The aim of this book therefore is to help you navigate your way around the best recruitment sites and make the most of online opportunities.

Andrea Semple
Matt Haig

CHAPTER 1

Getting Started

O ne of the areas where the so-called 'Internet revolution' has the biggest impact is in job-hunting and recruitment. Indeed, the Internet has evolved from being *one* way of seeking employment to become *the* best chance of finding relevant jobs. In fact, an increasing number of employers and recruitment agencies only advertise positions on the Internet in order to encourage candidates to apply online.

Despite this fact, many people remain sceptical about whether the Internet is right for their job-hunting efforts. Among the main concerns people have are:

◆ *Lack of technical knowledge.* As many job hunters remain wary of the Internet and computers in general they believe they do not have the necessary technical knowledge to search for jobs online. The fact is, however, that the Internet simplifies rather than complicates the job-hunting process.

◆ *Security.* One of the biggest fears people have is that any personal information they place online is not secure. As this book will explain, there are a number of cautionary measures which can be taken in order to ensure confidentiality is maintained.

◆ *Competition.* Many job hunters are intimidated by the sheer number of online candidates they are competing with.

◆ *Irrelevance.* There is a prevailing misconception that the Internet is only a useful job hunting tool for technology-related industries. While it used to be the case that only IT professionals could find work via the net, that situation has changed dramatically. The Internet is now a relevant job search aid for every career imaginable, from accountancy to zoo keeping.

While the purpose of this chapter is to explain how you should get started on your job search it is first a good idea to clarify exactly why the Internet is so important for employment hunters. After all, to carry out your Internet job-hunting with the right amount of enthusiasm, you need to be thoroughly convinced of the advantages. (A guide to the equipment and software you will need to get your online job-hunt underway is provided in the appendix to this book.)

The Advantages of Online Job-hunting

According to the Association of Graduate Recruiters (AGR) over two-thirds of employers seeking to attract candidates are using the Internet to do so. This indicates that the benefits the Internet provides for both employers and job-hunters are beyond dispute. The other advantages of job-hunting online include:

◆ *Cost.* The Internet helps save money for both job-hunters and employers, as it limits bureaucratic costs and reduces paperwork.

◆ *Time.* As well as saving money online job-seeking can also be more time-effective than using offline methods. It has certainly cut application response times from weeks to days or even hours.

◆ *Access.* Although many of the basic rules of recruitment remain the same the Internet gives you greater access to information on the job market.

◆ *Research.* Even if you are applying for a job via the postal service, the Internet can provide you with useful background information on a specific employer. As Angela Baron, from the Chartered Institute of Personnel and Development (CIPD), puts it:

'Not only will the Internet help you decide if this is really the employer for you, but it will arm you with knowledge during the application and interview stage.'

This view is supported by Charles Walker at recruitment agency Blue Arrow:

'There is now no excuse for turning up not knowing about the company interviewing you and the markets in which they operate.'

♦ *Convenience.* The Internet enables vacancies to come to you. Most of the major recruitment sites, including *Monster.co.uk, Reed.co.uk, Stepstone.co.uk* and *Workthing.com*, offer features that enable you to register with them and then have vacancies which meet your criteria e-mailed to you as soon as they come in.

If this isn't enough to persuade you of the benefits of job-hunting online consider the following facts:

♦ A recent survey from the Chartered Institute of Personnel and Development states that over 50 per cent of all employers are now using the Internet for recruitment purposes. Reed Executive put the figure at 68 per cent.

♦ According to research conducted by *The Guardian*, 78 per cent of white collar professionals have used the Internet to look for a job, while Universum claim that 83 per cent of graduates use Web sites to search for their first jobs.

♦ It is estimated that there are more than 200,000 UK-based jobs advertised on Internet recruitment sites at any one time.

♦ In 2000 over £20 million was spent on promoting 500 recruitment Web sites. Most of this promotion was aimed at employers.

♦ Ninety per cent of organisations believe they could benefit from using the Internet even more for recruitment purposes (according to a survey from human resource organisation, Cubiks).

Deciding on Your Dream Job

The Internet is the ultimate tool for deciding where exactly you want to be within the job market. It provides you with an almost infinite amount of information on the world of work.

Before you start your job-hunt in earnest, it is a good idea to surf the Web to see what is out there. Search engines, company Web sites, online recruitment sites and Internet-based career libraries can all be useful sources of information when you are deciding your dream job or career.

However, the Internet is not just a source of passive information. It also enables you to *interact* with career advisors and other job-seekers as there are thousands of online community forums centred around the subject of jobs and careers.

Although you may have a very clear idea of the type of job you are looking for, it is definitely worth keeping an open mind during the early stages of your job search.

The factors which will determine your dream job are as follows:

◆ *Your current situation.* As we shall see, your present situation has an inevitable influence on the sort of job you will be able to acquire.

◆ *Your experience.* Your past experience of work will have shaped your opinion of certain types of job.

◆ *Your talents.* When deciding your ideal job, you will need to think of where your skills and knowledge are best suited.

◆ *Your flexibility.* If you are willing to move to a different area or take up extra training, more jobs will be available to you.

◆ *The job market.* Your 'dream job' decision must, in part at least, be based on outside factors. The hard realities of the job market need to be taken into consideration.

◆ *Salary expectations.* The Internet can help you to determine how much you could be earning elsewhere. Some sites include salary calculators enabling you to work out how your current salary (if you have one) compares to other people within your industry.

Analysing Your Current Situation

To stand the best chance of getting the right job for you, you need to be able to analyse your current situation. After all, your present career status is clearly going to affect your future job prospects.

You will need to think about the advantages and disadvantages of your current situation, as well as the skills and experience you have acquired so far. When businesses want to review their situation they conduct a SWOT analysis to look at their present Strengths, Weaknesses, Opportunities and Threats. By carrying out a SWOT analysis of your own you will be able to get a clearer picture of where you are, and where potentially you can get to within the job market.

The Internet can also be a great source of help. As well as Web sites specialising in self-assessment tests (which are discussed in more detail further on in this chapter), there are a number of other online tools enabling you to analyse your present position. For instance, some recruitment sites (such as *Reed.co.uk*) include a salary calculator. By typing in your present annual salary in the calculator box, you can find out what you could be earning elsewhere in the country.

Also by using the Internet to find out information on your industry you can assess any trends or developments which may affect your present job. Furthermore, this can help you to spot any opportunities for the future, and help you to predict the ways in which you can benefit from them.

Steps to complete a SWOT Analysis

1. Create a work file on your computer to store all your work and job applications.

2. Make a list of all your work experience.

3. List all your current qualifications.

4. List your hobbies.

5. Decide on your dream job by using an online self-assessment site.

6. Research your dream job online. Check out information about the industry and company you would like to work for.

7. Decide if you will need any extra training.

8. Look at the job specification – and ask yourself if you are right for the company and job.

9. Complete a SWOT analysis using the information gained from the steps above.

Strengths	Weaknesses
Opportunities	Threats

Filling in the Gaps

Once you have conducted a SWOT analysis and reviewed your current situation, you may be able to locate gaps relating to your skills, education or experience. For instance, you may realise that you need to brush up on your computer skills in order to make yourself a more attractive prospect for employers.

Taking the time and effort to 'fill in the gaps' evident on your current CV can certainly pay off in the long term. Furthermore, as the job for life is now a thing of the past no one can afford to be complacent. By constantly seeking to bridge the gap between what you do know and what you should know, you will be investing in your own future and making your place within the job market more secure.

Here are some of the specific ways in which you can improve your job prospects within your chosen industry:

◆ *Gain experience.* If you are at university or college, or have just left, you may be lacking relevant work experience. Work experience ranges from unpaid employment and work shadowing, through temp work, to structured in-house training programmes. This sort of experience has two obvious benefits. Firstly, it will help to add real substance to your CV. Secondly, it will enable you to discover how the reality of a certain type of work matches your expectations.

◆ *Seek training.* There may be certain qualifications and skills required by your dream job which you currently lack. However, it is never too late to seek new training opportunities. The Internet can help you in your search for relevant training courses as there are a number of online course directories. For instance, Hot Courses (*www.hotcourses.com*) lists a huge selection of part and full-time courses of all levels. The UCAS (University and Colleges Admission Service) site (*www.ucas.ac.uk*) also has a course search facility where you can search by subject.

◆ *Improve your computer skills.* As the Internet is playing an ever more important role within commercial and other organisations, computer skills are increasingly valued by employers. You can either teach yourself or seek external training. As well as Hot Courses and UCAS, there are a number of other Web sites which may help you find out about computer training. For example, the Open University (*www.open.ac.uk*) offers a range of computer- and Internet-related courses. Technology companies such as Sun (*www.sun.co.uk*) and Cisco (*www.cisco.co.uk*) also run a series of different courses throughout the UK. Cyberia (*www.theinternetcompany.co.uk*) offers Internet training tailored to specific job functions (recent courses include Internet training for lawyers, teachers, accountants and health professionals).

Organising Your Time

Careful time management is absolutely essential when it comes to looking for work via the Internet. The sheer amount of online information means that you could spend a fortnight wading through Web sites and still not have discovered even half of the relevant vacancies out there.

Furthermore, despite being so incredibly vast, the Internet is a very fast-moving medium and new vacancy information arrives online every minute. (The Internet is reckoned to move at seven times the speed of normal time.)

Owing to the size and speed of the Internet, you will need to accept that you will never be able to find every piece of relevant information. In order to make your job-hunting as productive as possible you should also set yourself timescales and deadlines to stick to.

In addition, prioritising information and compiling your own directory of useful sites (using the 'Bookmark' or 'Favourite' option on your Web browser) can help you to get the most out of your Web surfing time.

Branding Yourself

While the Internet can increase the number of job opportunities available to you, it has also increased your competition. At any one time there will be literally thousands of CVs online, many of which will outline similar skills and qualifications to those you offer. Furthermore, as geographic location becomes ever less significant, you will find yourself competing with candidates from across the globe.

To differentiate your skills and experience from those of your fellow job-hunters, you will need to be able to market yourself effectively. The highly influential US management guru Tom Peters was the first person to come up with the concept of the 'Brand Called You'. 'I call the approach Me Inc.', Peters writes in his book *The Circle of Innovation*, 'You're Chairperson/CEO/Entrepreneur-in-Chief of your own professional service firm' (see Further Reading).

In the Internet age, success in the job market comes from paying attention to your own, individual brand. In other words, just as companies need to make an extra effort to distinguish themselves from their competitors, so too do job-hunters.

Here are some of the ways to ensure the right employers notice what you (or rather your 'brand') has to offer:

◆ *Play by the employer's rules.* In order to stand a chance with potential employers you must conform to their rules. If they want you to fill in an application form, don't send them a copy of your CV. Likewise, if they only accept online applications don't send your details via the post.

◆ *Make your CV stand out.* While your CV must follow a certain formula, you must also make sure it stands out. The more punchy and fact-filled, the better. It is important to be aware of the fact that many companies now use special scanning software to filter applications. Words which match the criteria specified in the job advert are usually more likely to get noticed.

◆ *Pick recruitment sites carefully.* If you decide to submit your CV to a recruitment site or agency you need to check out how the service works. Some recruitment sites send 'spam CVs' (i.e. CVs which haven't been asked for) to employers who may not even have heard of their service. This not only damages the brand name of the recruitment site, but also harms your own online brand identity.

◆ *Make applications relevant.* Unfortunately, many job-hunters seem to mistake the word 'application' for 'autobiography'. Employers are not interested in your life story, they only want to know about those aspects of your experience which are directly relevant to the job you are applying for.

◆ *Keep details up to date.* If your details are on a candidate database at a recruitment site, make sure they are kept up to date.

◆ *Research companies.* When you are applying to a company direct, it is important to have an in-depth knowledge of the organisation's culture and history. This can then be expressed in your application. After all, employers like to know that you have tailored your application to meet their requirements. The biggest mistake is to send out exactly the same application details to lots of employers simultaneously.

Assessing Your Abilities Online

Assessing your capabilities and deciding on a career direction can be a difficult process but there are a number of things that applicants can do in order to focus their thoughts. Traditionally undertaking work experience and speaking to careers advisors has proved useful. However, the Internet can also offer some valuable enlightenment.

Many of the major recruitment sites provide features aimed at helping candidates assess their own abilities. For instance, Reed includes two online self-assessment questionnaires, the Job Satisfaction Index and id60. The Job Satisfaction Index consists of 54 statements designed to help you make a choice about your future at work. The statements examine a number of areas which relate to your feelings about different aspects of your job. You can indicate whether you agree or disagree with each statement by selecting one of five options ranging from 'strongly disagree' to 'strongly agree'. Typical statements include:

◆ 'I sometimes think that I would be better suited to working for a different organisation.'

◆ 'I don't have time to talk to employment agencies.'

◆ 'There is a good working atmosphere in my organisation'.

Once you have responded to each of the 54 statements you click on the submit button and automatically receive a report on your Job Satisfaction Index.

The id60 test adopts a similar format although this time all the questions are based around your personality. Here are some of the statements you have to agree or disagree with:

- ◆ 'I find it easy to trust most people.'
- ◆ 'I tend to be rather lazy.'
- ◆ 'I nearly always manage to focus on the work in hand.'

Again, once you have completed the section, you can click on the Submit button to receive a report about what jobs your personality is best suited to.

Another more straightforward way to assess your suitability for a job is to look through the job databases at online recruitment sites. Sites such as Go Jobsite (*www.gojobsite.co.uk*) have industry profiles detailing different occupations, work conditions and salary expectations. You can then carry out a search to look at job descriptions to see if you have the qualities required. This can help you work out where your skills fit within the job market. Based upon suitability applicants may choose to improve upon skills and perhaps learn something new.

Online psychometric aptitude testing is also useful for assessing which industry may be most suitable for your personality.

Below are some more places on the Web which can help you assess your abilities and (as some sites refer to it) your ultimate 'career status':

ASE
www.ase-solutions.co.uk

As well as general career management information, this site includes a variety of online questionnaires and psychometric tests.

Assessment
www.assessment.com

Assessment features general information on psychometric tests and includes a personality questionnaire.

Career Storm
www.careerstorm.com

Your first impression of Career Storm may put you off. This US site initially seems rather complex and bizarre (it is designed visually as a sea journey). However, with a little perseverance, this site can prove to be a very real help in determining your goals. Career Storm includes practical tools that enable you to check, maintain or change the course of your career.

In line with the sea voyage theme, you are expected to spend as long as you need on each section and exercise (these are by no means quick tests). It is therefore probably best to print out certain sections or to save them on disk.

The Career Storm site is based on constructivist and constructionist theory. According to Career Storm, the constructivist career counselling theory 'emphasises the active role that you play in constructing your life. Constructionism, in turn, emphasises the interactive role of social relationships and examines how different relational influences shape your life'. Whether you decide to dismiss this as mumbo jumbo or not, the tests themselves are worth trying out.

C Web
www.cWeb.com

This US site features a variety of questions designed to help you think about your current job search strategy.

Emotional Intelligence
www.utne.com

Emotional Intelligence is a quality increasingly respected by employers. At this site you can test your emotional IQ as well as receive information on how to interpret your rating.

Hull University Careers
www.hull.ac.uk/careers

The University of Hull's online careers section is a mine of information on assessment procedures used by employers. The site covers assessment centres, aptitude and personality tests, aptitude surveys and psychometric testing.

Labour Mobility
www.labourmobility.com

If you are thinking about working abroad, Labour Mobility will prove to be a very useful site. It features a variety of information and tests relating to the qualities needed for working in another country.

Leaders Direct
www.leadersdirect.com

Leaders Direct is a UK-based site aimed at managers and team leaders. The site features a range of online questionnaires on areas such as values, self-esteem, assertiveness, anxiety, leadership, coping with change, promotion and stress. In addition, it includes valuable general information on assessment centres, management guidance, human resources, leadership and self-management. The site also hosts online forums on leadership and management, enabling you to communicate directly with other managers and leadership experts.

Monster
www.monster.com

The US version of the Monster job site includes a variety of assessment tools and quizzes for job hunters.

The Platinum Rule
www.platinumrule.com

The Platinum Rule is one of the most popular self-assessment sites on the Web and incorporates psychometric testing, attitude surveys and assessment centres as well as general career guidance. You can also take the 'Personality Style Quiz' which is designed to tell which of the four following personality categories you fall under: Director, Relater, Socializer or Thinker.

Total jobs
www.totaljobs.com

> This site features a very handy 'Career Health Check' which helps to find out what jobs are the perfect match for you. Once you have submitted your personal information, you are provided with an eight-page report detailing: the types of work you enjoy, your strengths and weaknesses in the working environment and the jobs you are most suited to.

More self-assessment sites can be located in the directory towards the end of this book.

Case Studies

Rajesh plans to change jobs

Rajesh is a primary school teacher in Nottingham. Although he teaches across a wide range of disciplines and enjoys his work immensely, he is interested in looking into special needs teaching. His wife has been offered a job in Newcastle which starts in three months and they are making the necessary arrangements to move there. Rajesh wants to find out if his personality would be suitable for special needs teaching which requires a lot of patience, as the pace of the learning is not easy to gauge. Teaching experience is required to achieve a post in special needs, but Rajesh may also require further training.

He decides to use one of the online self-assessment sites to ascertain if his personality and attitude are right for special needs. Rajesh use the Total Jobs site (*www.totaljobs.com*) Career Health Check to find out which jobs are the perfect match for him. He provides a lot of information about himself and his work experience and the Total Job site returns an eight-page report which concludes that Rajesh has a compassionate nature and is a perfect candidate for being a primary school teacher that could move into the special needs teaching field.

Trudy's SWOT analysis

Trudy is a 23-year-old business studies graduate from Belfast University. Having taken a gap year after leaving university (which she spent travelling around Australia) she has decided to start looking for a career. Trudy has no practical experience in any field. However, she is interested in a career which involves IT and marketing.

Trudy's strengths:

- Computer literate: able to use both PC and Mac, with a strong knowledge of Windows programs including Excel, Word and PowerPoint.
- Has used statistical packages such as SPSS.
- Internet literate – her business studies degree was heavily Internet focused.
- Easily adapts to new environments.
- A 2:1 degree.

Trudy's weaknesses:

- Lack of experience in any field – Trudy has never had a permanent or relevant job and undertook no work experience at university.

Trudy's opportunities:

- Belfast is a thriving 'Internet' recruitment area. The IT sector is actively looking for high calibre employees.

Trudy's threats:

- There are a lot more graduates with more work experience than her.
- Time is against her because degrees have shelf life.

Philip's SWOT analysis

Philip is an accountant who works at one of the largest accountancy companies in the City of London. He is 30 years old and has worked with the company for eight years. For the past two years his role has involved travelling to the company's partner offices in Dubai at least twice a month. Philip loves his job but dislikes the travelling and has explained this to his current employers. Unfortunately, his employers have said that his job must involve at least two monthly trips to Dubai. Philip is an excellent accountant and he wants to find a new job which does not involve any travel.

Philip's strengths:

- Philip is an excellent accountant and has an MBA in accountancy.
- Philip is a loyal member of staff – he has worked with the company for eight years.
- Philip is a member of the ACCA and has passed all his accountancy exams with flying colours.

Philip's weaknesses:

- Philip dislikes travel.
- Philip is unused to change. A company may be concerned at how

well he will cope with the change to a new company.

Philip's opportunities:

♦ Philip is a well trained accountant from a very prestigious accountancy company.

Philip's threats:

♦ Philip has been trained by a large accountancy company and perhaps he will not be open to new training or new ideas.
♦ Philip has no experience of working in the finance department of a big blue-chip company whereas many of the other candidates will have. _____

Checklist

To get your job-hunting efforts off on the right track you will need to:

♦ Be aware of the benefits of Internet job-seeking.
♦ Decide your dream job based on your current situation, your experience, your talents, the job market and salary expectations.
♦ Conduct a SWOT (Strengths, Weaknesses, Opportunities and Threats) analysis on your current situation.
♦ Fill any significant gaps in your experience or training.
♦ Make sure your job-search is timetabled.
♦ Brand yourself effectively.
♦ Assess your abilities online.

CHAPTER 2

Researching the Job Market

T he Internet is in many ways the ultimate research tool as it not only contains an infinite amount of information, but also offers tools which make locating the information you want a straightforward process. Search engines, meta-search sites (which are discussed later), discussion boards, online business directories, electronic newsletters and e-mail can all help you to research the job market. While later chapters will focus in depth on areas such as search engines and e-mail, the purpose of this chapter is to outline the reasons why research should be considered as the backbone of your job-search activity.

Research and the Internet

When it comes to online job-hunting, research is not just a question of locating vacancies. In order to find and secure the job you want, it will be necessary to search for more than job listings. Here are some of the other ways the Internet should be incorporated within your research activity:

- *Company research.* The Web can help you to find relevant information on a particular company you are interested in. This can help you to determine whether the company would be right for you (and vice versa).
- *Industry research.* You can use the Internet to find out which companies are the major players within a certain industry. The Internet can also provide you with up-to-the-minute news on the latest industry trends and developments which could affect your job chances.
- *Careers advice.* It can be a valuable source of career advice. As well as visiting careers sites, many companies and recruitment agencies can offer you valuable information.
- *Interview preparation.* Once you have secured an interview,

research becomes even more important. If you can show that you've done your homework on a company and the industry within which they operate you will have an automatic head start. Furthermore, interviewers have been known to ask questions such as 'Are you aware of what's happening in our profession at the present time?' If you can respond with a 'Yes' and then quickly qualify the answer, the employer will see you as a potentially valuable asset. Not only have you expressed a useful knowledge of the industry, but also (by implication) a great deal of enthusiasm for it as well.

◆ *General knowledge of the job market.* The Internet can also help you to gain a general knowledge of the current job market as a whole. Sites such as the *Financial Times'* FT.com (*www.ft.com*), the Confederation of British Industry (*www.cbi.org.uk*) and UK Business Park (*www.ukbusinesspark.co.uk*) all provide information on employment trends from a business perspective. Many of the main recruitment sites provide details of the job market tailored towards job-seekers.

◆ *Different areas.* If you are willing to move to a different area in order to secure your dream job, the Internet can help you to find information on the housing market, salary expectations and (if you are planning to move to a different country) the culture and climate.

◆ *Self-knowledge.* As you discovered in the last chapter, you can use the Internet to research yourself as self-assessment tests are available at various sites.

Planning Your Research

Successful research is always dependent on careful planning and organisation. This is particularly the case when it comes to the Internet, which, by its very nature, is unstructured. To conduct research effectively you will need to set SMART objectives.

SMART stands for Specific, Measurable, Achievable, Realistic and Timetabled:

◆ *Specific.* Before you start researching the job market, you need to work out what you *specifically* want to achieve. This means instead of making your objective 'to find the right job' you should specify what exactly constitutes 'the right job'.

◆ *Measurable.* Objectives should serve to help you measure the success of your research effort.

◆ *Achievable.* Do not overestimate what you can achieve.

◆ *Realistic.* Owing to the size and scaled nature of the Internet it is impossible to research every relevant aspect of the job market.

◆ *Timetabled.* As mentioned in the last chapter your job-hunting activity should be timetabled in order to keep your research on the right track.

Researching Companies

Once you know the name of a company or organisation you are interested in, your aim should be to log online and find out as much about them as possible. Too many people seem to believe that company research is an activity which should only be conducted after you have secured an interview.

However, although online research can pay off in an interview situation, you should start your research before you apply for a job in the first place, let alone secure an interview. After all, how can you tell if a job is for you unless you have a thorough understanding of the company?

If you know the Web address of a company, your first port of call should be their Web site (even if you don't know the Web address but know the company name you can usually find the site by typing the name into a search engine). Most company Web sites include an 'About Us' or 'Our Company' section which tell you the facts you want to know such as how long the company has been established, where they are based, the number of employees and so on. In addition, the Web site may include a 'Contact us' section which will enable you to e-mail a general enquiry. This can be a useful way of conducting primary (i.e. first-hand) research on a company. Some companies also include a 'Press Room' or 'Press Section'. These areas often feature press releases packed full of company facts.

Although a company Web site may seem to offer a comprehensive view of the company it represents, it never depicts the whole picture.

To get a true impression of a company or organisation you will have to stretch further afield.

The truth is out there

The fantastic thing about the Internet (for job-seekers at least) is that the truth is always out there. No matter how positive a company Web site may seem, if the image it conveys differs from the reality a corrective view will emerge elsewhere on the Web.

Employees with a complaint against a company can share their grievances with thousands of others in discussion groups by using a nickname to remain anonymous. In severe cases they can even vent their disdain by setting up 'anti-sites'. By typing in the name of a company into a discussion group search engine such as Google Groups (*http://groups.google.com*) you can often find out what employees have to say about their working conditions.

Obviously *all* employers claim to offer staff the best opportunities, but it's only by getting first-hand information from the employees themselves that you can know for sure if those claims are justified.

However, you can still tell a lot from the company site itself. For instance, a lengthy 'People' section which tells you about a cross-section of the staff (as opposed to just the board of directors), and an 'Investors in People' award are good signs to look out for.

Here are some useful sites to help you find out more information on a specific company:

◆ *Hoovers Online* (*www.hoovers.com*). Hoovers is a well respected site which includes information on large, international companies. It includes over 4,000 company profiles, 10,000 company financial reports and 12,000 company capsules (which consist of a brief overview and a link to the relevant company Web site). Job-seekers are entitled to a free trial subscription.

◆ *Companies Online* (*www.companiesonline.com*). Although the focus of this site is on US-based companies, many UK companies are included. In total, the site has information on over 100,000 public and private companies. Once you have registered (for free) you can receive details of annual sales, employee size, trade names, parent companies, contact names, contact titles and e-mail addresses.

♦ *UK Business Park* (*www.ukbusinesspark.co.uk*). The UK Business Park has information on thousands of UK companies, which you can search by company name.

♦ *News Now* (*www.newsnow.co.uk*). An indepth newspaper search is available here.

More useful sites can be found in the directory towards the end of this book.

Researching industries

As well as finding information on individual companies, you can also use the Internet to improve your knowledge of an industry area. This can help you in a number of ways. It can arm you with useful knowledge for an interview, help you to assess whether the industry is right for you, and give you an idea of what you can expect once you are part of it.

The sort of information which could prove useful includes the following:

♦ *Economic forecasts.* Predictions regarding the economic future of an industry clearly have an impact on employment prospects.

♦ *New developments.* If you are applying for a job it is always a good idea to express your knowledge of any relevant new industry developments.

♦ *Key players.* Information on the individuals, companies and brands which carry the most weight within an industry may prove useful in an interview situation.

To find specific information you will need to visit trade Web sites as well as general business sites. The Yahoo! UK Business and Economy directory (*www.yahoo.co.uk/business_and_economy*) is a good place to start your hunt for industry facts and figures.

Visiting Recruitment Sites

Although recruitment sites are an obvious place to look for vacancies, they can also help your research in other ways. As you will discover in Chapter 4 many of these sites can provide detailed information on the job market in general as well as on specific industries. They also often provide useful careers advice relating to areas such as writing a CV, preparing for an interview, filling in application forms and so on.

In fact many recruitment and job sites act more as job-search 'portals' than anything else. In other words, they can lead you to various other useful resources on the Web through their link pages. This saves you the problem of having to locate a list of useful sites for yourself.

Evaluating Information

Although the Internet provides you with access to a wide range of information relating to companies and the job market, it does not usually give you a way of valuing information.

The fact that anyone can post content onto the Web is therefore a mixed blessing. It means that you will often come across Web sites which contradict each other and which offer conflicting advice. Which do you believe? How should you differentiate between information sources?

Unfortunately, there is no one method of distinguishing between the good, the bad and the ugly information on the Web. After all, the value of information is clearly dependent on the type of job you are looking for. However, there are a number of ways in which you can fine tune your research in order to concentrate on quality. These include:

◆ *Looking at the country of origin.* If you are looking for a job in the UK, the advice offered by British career sites is likely to be more directly relevant to you than that found at a US or Australian Web site.

◆ *Using directories and search engines compiled by humans.* While many search engines rely on software to place sites on their indexes, a growing number of sites are depending on human judgement. For instance, Yahoo! and Lycos now both use a panel of experts to rank sites according to the quality of their content.

◆ *Seeking recommendations.* Fellow job-hunters are often willing to offer their recommendations of useful sites.

Online consumer forums such as Epinions (*www.epinions.com*) and Ciao (*www.ciao.com*) are particularly useful as they often include Web site reviews.

◆ *Look for third party approval.* Many sites feature awards or seals of recommendation they have received from trade organisations or industry bodies. For UK sites which require personal information from visitors look for a Which? Online or Truste Scheme logo. Both of these companies endorse sites which are secure and trustworthy.

◆ *Check for sales jargon.* Generally speaking, sites which are selling a product or a service have a different agenda to those which serve only to provide information.

Finding People in Similar Jobs

One of the best forms of research comes from finding and contacting people in similar jobs to the one you are applying for. This is particularly useful if you have no first-hand experience of this type of job yourself.

There are a number of ways in which you can find employees online. You can search discussion groups by typing in keywords based on the industry or company you are interested in, you can use a people finder service such as WhoWhere.com or HotBot's People Search (although these services are only really useful if you already now the person's name) or you can visit company Web sites and take down the contact details of relevant members of staff.

Although people may be too busy to provide you with lengthy information, some will be more than happy to answer short and simple enquiries (especially if they are already an active member of a discussion forum). Again, the sort of questions you ask will depend entirely on the job you are interested in. However, the area you want to find information on will probably include job security, what the job actually encompasses, salary expectations and maybe even the questions you should ask at the interview (see below).

Researching for an Interview

When you have secured an interview, you will need to brush

up on your knowledge about a company and its industry. This will help to improve your level of confidence and enable you to answer any tricky questions. One of the most frequently asked interview questions of all is: 'So, why do you want to work for us?' Most candidates when faced with this question resort to vague answers along the lines of 'Because it seems like a stimulating environment' or 'Because it will help me to fulfil my potential'.

Although these answers are not *wrong* as such, they are telling the interviewer nothing. If you can respond to this question with some genuine insight into what the company does or is about, you are far more likely to make a positive impression. After all, employers are after people with a genuine interest in their company rather than those whose only motivation is their monthly pay cheque.

Obviously the sort of research you do depends on the position you are applying for. For instance, if you are being interviewed for a job in the marketing department it will help you to know if there are any new product or service launches in the pipeline. Likewise, if you are after a position in the financial department you should research the company's financial reports.

The other way the Internet can help you research for an interview is by providing you with useful interview tips. A number of career and recruitment sites include features on how to handle interview questions and the golden rules of 'interview etiquette'.

At the time of writing the recruitment sites Reed.co.uk, Go Jobsite (*www.gojobsite.co.uk*) and Major Players (*www.majorplayers.co.uk*) all featured articles on interview techniques. Furthermore, many online careers services (particularly university services) can provide tailored advice relating to the specific position you are applying for.

Conducting research via e-mail

While the Web may be the most obvious Internet research tool at your disposal, e-mail can also assist you research efforts. You can use e-mail to make general enquiries at company Web sites, recruitment sites and other online careers services.

The advantages of e-mail as a research tool include the following:

◆ *Cost.* You can make hundreds of enquiries via e-mail at little or no expense.

◆ *Convenience.* E-mail enquiries are convenient for both you and the recipient. You can send them at any time you like, and the recipient can choose to respond when they want. To respond all they need to do is click on the 'reply' button.

◆ *Speed.* E-mails arrive in the recipient's inbox a few seconds after you click 'send' (in theory at least). Furthermore, the convenience of replying often ensures a speedy response.

◆ *Multiplicity.* You can send out the same enquiry to a lot of companies simultaneously. However, when you do this make sure that you place all the e-mail addresses in the 'Bcc': (Blind carbon copy) box. This will ensure that each address remains hidden from the other recipients.

◆ *Primary research.* As e-mail enables you to contact people directly, it can help you to conduct primary research directly relevant to your job-hunt.

When you are sending e-mail enquiries to companies it is a good idea to try and keep each message as short as possible. Longer messages are less likely to be read, and therefore less likely to be responded to.

Case studies

Trudy's SMART objectives

Trudy's SMART objective is as follows:

> To gain a work placement with an Internet marketing company in Belfast for one month by the end of July.

Specific: Trudy's objective is specific because it states what type of company she wants to work in and where. It could be more specific if she had stated what type of role she would like to gain experience in and what size company she would prefer. A large Internet marketing company would have different job roles that may be suitable for Trudy. She will have to study companies to better understand their structure and the types of jobs they offer.

Measurable: The objective can be measured.

Achievable: Trudy is uncertain whether this work placement can be achieved because she does not know if Internet marketing companies in Belfast offer work placements. However, most companies are willing to hear from people who are interested in such placements.

Realistic: The objective is realistic because Trudy has given herself a three-month timescale.

Timetabled: By the end of July is Trudy's timetable deadline.

Philip's SMART objectives
Philip's SMART objective is as follows:

> To find an accountancy job (which involves no travel) for a multinational corporation in London with a salary package of between £40,000 and £45,000 by the end of September.

Specific The objective is specific. He is looking for an accountancy job for a multinational organisation. It could be even more specific if he knew what market sector he was looking at or particular company names within it. An Internet search will be able to help him with this.

Measurable: All aspects of the objective can be measured. It has to be an accountancy job for a multinational company and he has even set himself a financial target. Also, Philip had included a time deadline (he wants the job by the end of September).

Achievable: The objective is achievable because Philip has allowed himself a realistic time period within which to proceed through the job process.

Realistic: The objective is realistic because Philip is in a similar job earning a similar amount of money.

Timetabled: Philip has set himself a timescale of the end of September.

Philip decides to research blue-chip multinational companies based in London and uses Hoovers Online to try to see which companies would be the most suitable targets. Hoovers has a huge database and Philip decides to narrow his search to the mobile communication industry. Philip is very interested in this industry and feels that it will provide many future opportunities. He finds company overviews of Orange, BT Cellnet, Vodafone and One2One.

Rajesh researches Newcastle

Rajesh is concerned about moving to Newcastle because he does not know it very well and is unsure of the best area to live in the city. He decides to use the Internet to find out a little more about Newcastle.

His first stop is Newcastle's online tourist information centre. He gains some general knowledge from the tourist information centre and decides to find out more. He searches the Internet for Web sites that provide information on particular areas and finds a Web site called Up My Street (*www.upmystreet.com*). The site describes itself as the 'real-life guide to your neighbourhood'. Rajesh discovers local services and stores, property prices, council records and police crime figures for the area.

Checklist

In order to research the job market thoroughly you should:

- ◆ Set SMART (Specific, Measurable, Achievable, Realistic, Timetabled) objectives.
- ◆ Research individual companies.
- ◆ Use business directories.
- ◆ Seek relevant information on the latest developments affecting the industry (or industries) you are interested in.
- ◆ Seek careers advice online (at recruitment sites and other career services).
- ◆ Learn to differentiate between valuable and irrelevant information.
- ◆ Contact people in similar jobs.
- ◆ Think of the questions you could be asked in the interview situation.
- ◆ Use e-mail to conduct primary research.

CHAPTER 3

Finding Vacancies

The Internet provides you with a variety of ways to find relevant job vacancies. To maximise your chances of finding the right job, you should use a combination of methods. This chapter provides a general overview of each method, while Chapter 4 focuses in greater depth on using online recruitment sites and agencies – which are the most popular ways in which job-hunters are locating suitable vacancies.

Visiting Company Web Sites

Most companies promote their internal vacancies on line at their own Internet sites even if they have used other promotional vehicles such as newspapers, job-search sites or magazines. Furthermore, the vacancy information posted on the company's Web site is likely to be a lot more detailed than that found elsewhere.

If you have a specific company in mind, the best option would be to visit their Web site and look for a job section to see if they have any relevant vacancies. If you know the name of the company you are interested in but are unsure of their Web site address, your best bet is to type the company name into one of the major search engines (Google, Alta Vista, Excite, etc.). As well as using search engines you could also try online business directories such as Yell (*www.yell.co.uk*) and Europages (*www.europages.com)*. Both these sites enable you to search by location and type of company. The UK Business Park (*www.ukbusinesspark.co.uk*) enables you to search through companies which are currently recruiting in its 'Opportunities for Employment' section.

Web sites have a link to the job section on the home page, called 'Jobs', 'Opportunities' or 'Vacancies'. If there is not a direct link you should be able to find the job section via an

'About This Company' (or similar) link. The more advanced sites provide the opportunity to forward your CV to a central database which matches your profile to a relevant vacancy.

Below are some examples of companies that promote vacancies on their Web sites. This will give you an idea of what you can expect to find at the job sections of some of the larger UK and international Web sites (many more can be found in the Directory at this end of this book).

Amazon
www.amazon.co.uk

Amazon's 'Join our staff' section lists the departments (such as Books, DVD and Video, Legal and Marketing) that are currently recruiting staff. It also provides a brief overview of each job with relevant contact details. If there are no suitable job vacancies, Amazon allows you to e-mail your CV to the Amazon.com recruitment database which assesses your suitability for future vacancies.

Bass
www.bass.co.uk

The Bass Web site provides general information on the Bass Graduate Recruitment Scheme and gives relevant contact information of staff who can help with further enquiries. At the time of writing Bass was creating a system that will be able to capture information from people interested in a career with the company.

BBC
www.bbc.co.uk

The BBC has a 'Jobs' section clearly indicated on its home page. The jobs area lists all current vacancies and includes information such as job title, hours, location and details of how to apply. There is a search option available which can be searched by 'job type', 'job location' or keyword.

The jobs section is also a useful source of information for training opportunities and schemes (such as the 'Production Trainee Scheme', 'Broadcast Journalist Trainee Scheme' and 'New Media Trainee Scheme'). There is also an FAQ section and an option to subscribe to the BBC's weekly staff newspaper called *Ariel* which details all vacancies and features.

GlaxoSmithKlein
www.gsk.com

Glaxo Smith Klein has a search facility on its job section (users can search by country, area of interest or job type). Glaxo Smith Klein offers the opportunity of applying online by either filling in their online CV or by copying the text of your CV into a specified area.

IBM
www.ibm.com

The IBM site offers world-wide job vacancies on its Web site. Job searches can be narrowed down by country or region and then by job positions such as 'experienced professional jobs' and 'current graduate openings'. Their vacancy details include information regarding position type, location of job, a job description and the necessary skills required. The IBM job vacancy section also offers a 'Life @ IBM' overview which is a useful insight (especially for anyone applying for a job) into the company.

KPMG
www.kpmg.co.uk

The KPMG Web site's career section includes a bulletin board that lists current vacancies, KPMG news and a careers calendar. The site also provides a profile of a KPMG employee which shows what life at KPMG is actually like. There is an online application form and a job search facility available. KPMG also offers the opportunity to register for e-mail alerts of new positions that match your search criteria.

LastMinute.com
www.lastminute.com

Would-be candidates must scroll down the lastminute.com vacancy list to look for suitable jobs. The company provides information about the job role including main duties and responsibilities and the type of person they are looking for. Applicants can only apply via e-mail.

Lego
www.lego.com

Lego's Web site has one of the most straightforward and instantly accessible job sections on the Web. It lists all vacancies via country and provides an overview of the job with contact e-mail addresses to send your CV to.

Lush
www.lush.co.uk

The cosmetics company, Lush, has a search option available which lets users view all vacancies or by specific career or by job type. A brief overview of the job and relevant contact details are given.

Microsoft
www.microsoft.com

The Microsoft job section is accessed via the 'Information' link on the main site's homepage. This provides in-depth overviews of job roles available and the type of people they are seeking. Applications can only be made by CV.

Motorola
www.motorola.com

Motorola has created another Web site called Motorola Careers (*www.motorolacareers.com*) which can be either accessed direct or via the 'About Motorola' link on its home page. The Motorola careers site has a search facility that can narrow your search by keyword, job function, location or experience level. Applicants can submit their CV online irrespective of whether they have a suitable job at the moment. The information is then forwarded to a 'global candidate database' where a 'hiring manager' matches your skills and interests to the right opportunity.

Price Waterhouse Coopers
www.pwcglobal.co.uk

> The PriceWaterhouseCoopers Web site provides job-seekers with information on undergraduate placements (such as gap years and summer vacations), graduate placements (such as different career options and qualifications required) and experienced vacancies (jobs available throughout the company).
>
> The PWC Web site has a downloadable PDF application form which can be printed out and posted to the company.

Tesco
www.tesco.co.uk

> Tesco's Web site contains graduate recruitment information with a general overview of the graduate selection process.

Thorntons
www.thorntons.co.uk

> The Thorntons job section is very simple and easy to use. A general overview of jobs is given and an online application form is available.

Looking at Online Newspapers and Journals

Online national newspapers

> Most of the national newspapers' job sections have online counterparts. At most of their sites, vacancies are updated more frequently than they are in their offline versions. Furthermore, some newspaper sites include more vacancy information than the job supplements they represent. Also, unlike many equivalent sites in the US, most UK newspaper sites do not require you to submit personal information or to become a site member in order to access the job listings.
>
> Below is a list of newspapers with their Web addresses and the work sectors they cover:

Daily Telegraph
www.telegraph.co.uk

The *Daily Telegraph* has two job vacancy Web sites, Business File and Appointments Plus.

◆ Business File (*www.businessfile-online.com*)

The Business File Web site is aimed squarely at job-hunters seeking top management and board-level positions. As a result the site exclusively offers appointments for £55,000 and over.

A personalised appointments search is available, although registration is required.

◆ Appointments Plus (*www.appointments-plus.co.uk*)

The Appointments Plus site is where the bulk of positions advertised in the newspaper can be found. The search facility enables you to either conduct a general search or to search by industry.

The work areas that are covered include 'Catering and Leisure', 'Computing' and 'General Administration'.

The Financial Times
www.ft.com

The *Financial Times* career section is called Career Point and it has access to hundreds of job advertisements. The four sections to the FT Career Point are as follows:

1. *The Job Search section.* This is the only area at the FT site which includes vacancy listings. The vacancies are divided into categories such as 'Agriculture', 'Building and Construction' and 'Tourism and Leisure'.

   There is also the option for searching companies according to the following criteria:

   – Start-up
   – Small/Medium Co.
   – Large Co.
   – Multinational
   – Public Sector

2. *Career advice.* As well as its database of vacancies the FT site includes a useful career advice section.

3 *World of Work.* The World of Work section features articles on employment issues.

4. *MBA News.* As the title suggests, MBA News provides the latest information on MBA courses.

The Guardian Jobs Unlimited
www.jobsunlimited.co.uk
www.guardianunlimited.co.uk

The *Guardian*'s Web site was one of the first UK sites to offer comprehensive vacancy listings. It remains one of the most popular sites among online job-seekers. The site has a very user-friendly job-search facility and is recognized by employers as one of the best ways to attract suitable candidates. The Guardian Jobs section is divided into the following subsections: 'Media and Sales', 'Education', 'IT and Telecoms', 'Secretarial', 'Marketing and PR', 'International', 'Science and Technology' and 'New Media'.

The search facility enables you to search by keyword and it is also easy to browse by job sector.

However, perhaps the most useful aspect of this site is the Career Manager facility which finds suitable jobs for you and stores ads you like.

The Scotsman
www.scotsman.com

The Careers and Education section of *Scotsman.com* is an online resource for schools, universities and those seeking recruitment news. The section features a Job Finder facility which searches extensive lists of vacancies. Search criteria is by sector, location or salary, or by typing in a relevant keyword. Categories that are covered include 'Engineering, Technical, IT', 'Public and Voluntary' and 'Sales, Marketing and Media'.

The Times
www.thetimes.co.uk/appointments

The Times Appointments section provides full details of the vacancies listed in *The Times* newspaper. To assist you in your search you can choose to use the dropdown menu, a keyword search or a combination of the two. The site requires a login name to upload your CV or to use a personal folder. *The Times* also has a separate job site for the *Times Education Supplement* (*www.job.tes.co.uk*).

Regional and local press

If you are looking for a local job your online local and regional press is a good place to start (a full list can be found in the Directory at the end of this book). It may come as some surprise but most regional newspaper sites provide comprehensive job listings. However, as the majority of the local and regional newspaper online job sections are updated by Fish4Jobs (*www.fish4jobs.co.uk*) it makes sense to start your search for local jobs here.

The link on the Fish4Jobs homepage called Newspaper Links does exactly what it says – it links to all the local newspapers that it works with. Offering between 25,000 and 30,000 jobs throughout the country from the UK's regional press. Fish4Jobs is the largest service of its kind. As Fish4Jobs is represented in around 80 per cent of the UK's regional press (more than 800 daily and weekly newspapers) it is more than likely to cover the area where you are looking to work.

Fish4Jobs lets you search for jobs in a variety of ways. You can search by job title (there are over 100 job titles ranging from Accountant to Waitress), working option (part-time, contract, consultant, etc.), job category, salary or keyword.

The London *Evening Standard* has a Web site devoted entirely to vacancy information called **Big Blue Dog** (*www.bigbluedog.com*)

You can also access the online versions of regional newspapers at the following Yahoo! address: *http://uk.dir.yahoo.com/Regional/Countries/United_Kingdom/News_and_Media/Newspapers/*

Using Trade Web Sites

Trade Web sites (an extensive list is provided in the Directory at the end of this book) are either sites set up by a professional organisation or by industry magazines or journals. Although the Web sites of professional organisations rarely include a vacancy database, they often include discussion forums. As is discussed elsewhere in this chapter (see 'Listening to word of mouth online') discussion areas can be a great source of vacancy information.

Web sites representing trade magazines, on the other hand, often include a classified job listings section. Many employers prefer to advertise with trade magazines as the adverts are cheaper and more targeted than they are in the national newspaper supplements. After all, the average reader of *PR Week* is likely to be a lot more interested in PR vacancies than the average reader of a national newspaper.

Also, if an employer has advertised in both a national newspaper and a trade publication they will probably prefer candidates who spot the ad via the trade title. The reason employers give for this is that it shows the applicant is interested enough in the industry to buy or subscribe to its publication.

Media UK (*www.mediauk.com*) and Yahoo!'s UK directory are good places to find information on, and links to, trade Web sites.

Online Career Libraries

There are a number of online career libraries in the UK which provide vacancy information. General public library Web sites often include a 'Careers' section providing vacancy details alongside careers advice. University Web sites are also good places to look as they typically include a 'jobs and careers' area. For instance, the University of Hull's online careers library (*www.hull.ac.uk/careers*) provides vacancy details for graduate jobs throughout the UK.

Other online libraries can be found at:

◆ **Book a Course** (*www.bookacourse.com*);
◆ **The British Library** (*www.bl.uk*);

◆ **London Business School Library** (www.lbs.ac.uk/library).

Listening to Word of Mouth Online

One of the unique features of the Internet is its ability to generate word-of-mouth, or 'word-of-*mouse*', awareness. As everyone on the Internet is connected, it is much easier to find out information from people than it is offline. Whereas in the 'real world' you may know around ten people you could contact for vacancy information, on the Internet grapevine you can get to hear what anyone has to say.

As we shall see in the next chapter many of the major recruitment sites incorporate huge online discussion forums where job-seekers and employers can exchange information with each other. You can also search through the Usenet job discussion groups at the Google site (*http://groups.google.com*). Often news of a vacant position appears here weeks before it is officially advertised at a recruitment site or in a newspaper's jobs supplement.

There are two ways you can use these forums to find out about vacancies. You can either search by keyword for vacancy news relating to the industry and geographical area you are interested in working in, or you can take the more proactive approach and post questions asking where you can find out about upcoming vacancies.

Helping jobs find you

Many of the major recruitment sites such as **Go Jobsite** (*www.gojobsite.co.uk*) and **Reed** (*www.reed.co.uk*) provide an e-mail service – enabling, in effect, jobs to come to you. These services allow job-hunters to sit back and wait for relevant opportunities to be delivered straight to their desktop. At Go Jobsite full descriptions are e-mailed out for every job.

Some of the more specialist recruitment sites also offer e-mail services. For instance, **Major Players** (*www.majorplayers.co.uk*), which specialises in marketing and new media jobs, offers an e-mail alert service which is updated on a daily basis. Candidates simply select the industry they are interested in, such as advertising, provide their name and e-mail address, and then wait for news on the latest relevant jobs to arrive in their inboxes.

One of the most popular of the e-mail job finder services is Reed's Job Sleuth service. This service can automatically send you relevant vacancy information to your e-mail address or via text message to your mobile phone. To activate Job Sleuth candidates need to register and sign in. When candidates register they can choose how and when they receive alerts and also specify their search criteria. Job-seekers can choose as many as three separate Job Sleuths with different criteria, so whatever you are interested in you can find out about the latest vacancies the moment they appear.

Other recruitment web sites that offer an e-mail service include the following:

City jobs
www.cityjobs.co.uk

This site specialises in Financial, Media and IT jobs.

Compurecruit
www.uk.compurecruit.com

Specialising in IT jobs.

GAAP Web
www.gaapweb.com

Specialising in finance and accountancy.

Jobline
www.jobline.co.uk

Their 'Matchmail' system is very useful.

Jobs Network
www.jobsnetwork.co.uk

Covers all job sectors.

Job Pilot
www.jobpilot.co.uk

> Covers all job sectors including overseas jobs.

Job Search
www.jobsearch.co.uk

> The selection criteria also include location.

Monster
www.monster.co.uk

> Covers all job sectors.

Workthing
www.workthing.com

> Registration is very quick.

> More information on recruitment sites can be found in the next chapter.

Finding Freelance Vacancies

> The growing role of the Internet in the work environment has led to an increase not only in teleworking but also in freelance opportunities. The Internet has made contract-based work more convenient and easier to come by, as freelancers now have a greater knowledge of the potential projects out on the market.

> The main incentive of freelance work is increased earnings. It is now common knowledge that freelancers can earn much more than their permanently employed counterparts. Leona Siaw, a recruitment consultant for the Staffing Solutions Division of application development company Midas IT Services, admitted in an *Internet* magazine article that, 'Contractors can demand significantly more than permanent workers. For example, an IT contractor with as little as two years' experience can earn over £60 an hour.'

> However, freelance work is not without its drawbacks. The increased flexibility (and pay) freelancing brings with it is offset

by instability. There's no pension scheme or holiday pay, and a lot of self-motivation is involved.

On balance, though, freelancers tend to agree that the advantages outweigh the disadvantages. As James Davies, a freelance Web designer based in Edinburgh, puts it, 'Freelancing puts everything in your own hands, which is ultimately very liberating.'

There are many Web sites which are dedicated to helping freelancers find work. They include the following:

EFreelancers
www.efreelancers.co.uk

This site is one of the largest open online databases of freelance professionals in the UK. Users are able to search the database to find the right services and providing you are a freelance professional, you can add or amend your details at any time you require. Once a company has used the service of a freelancer included on the database, they are encouraged to add a reference to help other employers make an informed choice. The freelance occupations covered in the database include accountants, architects, consultants, copywriters, designers, editors, engineers, journalists, legal professionals, musicians, new media professionals, photographers, secretaries and translators. The site also features a useful discussion area intended to create a healthy community of UK freelance professionals.

Elance
www.elance.com

Elance calls itself 'The Premier Global Services Marketplace' and is aimed at qualified freelance service professionals and those companies looking for their services. Although the site emphasises its 'global' reach it must be admitted that the majority of projects are US based. However, the Internet enables professionals based in the UK to work remotely for a US business. The way the site works is simple. Companies post their projects, providers of professional services then place their bids (and name their price) and the company chooses the freelancer they want. With sections called 'Buy Services' and 'Provide Services' the site caters equally for companies and freelancers. It covers a wide range of industries, including areas such as 'Accounting and Finance', 'Administrative Support', 'Business Strategy', 'Graphic Design', 'Legal', 'Software and Technology', 'Web Design and Development' and 'Writing and Translation'. The site provides a community section which offers valuable networking opportunities, as well as a 'My Elance' feature enabling you to personalise the site to meet your own requirements.

Freelance Informer
www.freelanceinformer.com

Freelance Informer is an UK-based site specifically aimed at IT freelancers. The site provides a convenient search facility enabling you to search its vast freelance job database by location, keyword and job type. As well as the database, Freelance Informer offers useful news articles and features along with a handy 'First Timers' section.

Freelance Journalist
www.freelancejournalist.co.uk

The main focus of the Freelance Journalist site is its UK directory of freelance journalists which provides journalists with the opportunity to create their own Web page on the site. As well as freelance writers, there are sections for editors (and subeditors), photographers, broadcasters and graphic designers. According to the site's home page the directory receives 10,000 hits per month and features prominently on the major search engines.

Journalism
www.journalism.co.uk

The Journalism.co.uk site is not aimed solely at freelance work seekers as it includes vacancies for full-time, in-house positions. However, its freelance section is one of the best places for professional freelance journalists to find out about suitable positions.

Local Freelance Sites

There are also a number of locally based freelance sites. For instance, Creative Freelance (*www.creative-freelance.org.uk*) provides a showcase for the work of creative freelance professionals based in Ipswich. Among its members are freelance professional illustrators, artists, writers, graphic designers and craftspeople. To find your local freelance site visit a major search engine such as Google (*www.google.com*) and type in keywords based on your freelance occupation and geographical location.

Create Your Own Freelance Site

Another option popular among freelancers is to create a Web site promoting their skills and experience. This is a good way of attracting the attention of employers searching the Web, especially if you can achieve a high ranking on the main search engines and directories.

Many people are put off from creating their own Web site because they feel it will involve too much time and effort. However, the emergence of straightforward Web authoring tools, referred to as WYSIWYG ('What You See Is What You Get') packages, means that anyone can create their own Web page or site. WYSIWYG packages such as Microsoft's Front Page, Adobe's Go Live and Macromedia's Dreamweaver enable you to set up a code (the programming language used to build Web pages) on your behalf. These packages provide design templates, offering ready-made design elements such as buttons, banners and icons. Although this software may cost money, it is often available for free as part of a CD on the cover of Internet magazines so keep a look out (this is a popular way for software manufacturers to promote awareness of their product before they release an upgraded version).

So, what makes a successful freelance site? Well, obviously the answer to this question depends on the type of freelance work the site owner does, and the type of employer they are trying to attract. However, there are some common pieces of information all freelance sites should include, as follows:

◆ *Contact details.* This should include your name, address, telephone number(s), fax number and e-mail address.

◆ *Work overview.* A general overview of the type of work you do and the services you provide should be included on the home page.

◆ *Work examples.* If applicable, it is a good idea to provide actual examples, or at least case studies, of the sort of work you have done for other employers.

◆ *Relevant links.* Relevant links to previous and/or current employers may help visitors to get a better understanding of your work.

◆ *References.* Employer references will help add weight to any positive claims made about yourself.

Promoting Your Site

The main way to promote your Web site when it is up and running is via the main search engines. Although there is no rock solid way to ensure a high search ranking, there are a number of ways you can improve your chances. These include:

◆ *Keywords.* Search engines work on a keyword basis. In other words Internet users type in relevant words and phrases in order to find the sites they want. By incorporating the keywords relevant employers are likely to type into search engines into your home page you are more likely to be picked up by those search engines. You can also include keywords in special instructions (called meta-tags) within your site's HTML code.

◆ *Links.* Search engines like popular sites. One of the ways in which they assess a Web site's popularity is by looking at the number of sites linking to it. Therefore it makes sense to try and arrange link partnerships with other relevant sites. Links also provide another way for employers to reach your site.

◆ *Fresh content.* Updating the content of your site on a regular basis is another way to keep search engines interested.

◆ *Submitting your site.* If you don't want to wait for search engines to find your site submit your site personally by filling in the submission pages of the main search sites. This will enable you to speed up the whole search ranking process.

For more information on designing and promoting your Web site visit **Wilson Web** (*www.wilsonweb.com*), a US site which since 1995 has been one of the leading resources on Web marketing and site creation. It also provides a valuable newsletter *Web Marketing Today*, which now boasts over 100,000 subscribers.

Another great source of information can be found at **Internet Works** (*www.iwks.com*). As well as providing useful tips and advice on building and marketing Web sites, it also features a comprehensive directory of UK-based Web site designers.

Case studies

Trudy searches for local Internet marketing jobs

Trudy achieved her aim of completing work experience in an Internet marketing company in Belfast and she decides to start looking for a paid job in that field.

Trudy is looking for an Internet marketing related job in Belfast, so she decides to use a local Web site to see if there are any suitable vacancies. She accesses the *Belfast Telegraph* Web site (she found the site on the front cover of the paper). She clicks on the job finder section which has two relevant sections for her: 'Graduates/Employers' and 'Register here for an IT job'. She chooses the 'Register here for an IT job' link which takes her to a page that explains how the IT sector in Northern Ireland is thriving and how the industry is actively seeking new recruits. There is an e-mail job service which will send her an e-mail announcement whenever a relevant IT job is received.

Philip uses the Orange Web site

Philip is looking for an accountancy job with a multinational company. He has heard positive information about the company Orange. He logs onto the Internet to try to locate the site. Philip does not know the Web site's address so he searches at the Yahoo.co.uk site. He uses the following keywords: 'orange mobile communications'. The top matching result is a direct link to the **Orange Web site** (*www.orange.co.uk*). There is no general job section on the homepage but he looks in the 'About Orange' section and finds a 'Jobs at Orange' link. The link provides him with an e-mail address to send a covering letter and CV to.

Rajesh locates the online version of the *Times Educational Supplement*
Rajesh is a primary school teacher planning to move into the special needs teaching area when he moves to Newcastle. Rajesh wants to research what the job field is like in Newcastle and also what training is available in the North East.

He knows one of the best resources for education jobs is the *Times Educational Supplement*. Instead of buying the newspaper very week he finds the *Times Educational Supplement* Web site (*www.tes.co.uk*) via the Google search engine – on typing in 'times educational supplement' the site is top of the search. When he arrives at the site he links to the job section (*www.tesjobs.co.uk*) and searches for special needs in Newcastle. He is surprised to find 56 relevant jobs available in the area. Rajesh signs up to the e-mail alert service available from the site which means that he will receive all relevant jobs as soon as they are posted.

Find out how Rajesh searches for training schemes in Chapter 6.

Checklist

To find relevant vacancies online you will need to try a combination of the following techniques:

- ◆ Visit the Web sites of companies you are interested in.
- ◆ Browse through the job sections of online newspapers.
- ◆ Visit trade Web sites (of both trade organisations and journals).
- ◆ Use online career libraries.
- ◆ Search online forums.
- ◆ Subscribe to recruitment sites' e-mail services.

Chapter 4

Using Online Recruitment Sites

The Internet has completely redefined the recruitment process. Recruitment sites can now offer job-hunters a greater choice of vacancies than ever before. Likewise, job-hunters can shop around for the right recruitment site with much greater ease. This means that recruitment sites are having to add value to their traditional services in order to meet the demands of the net-savvy job-seeker.

There are two main types of recruitment sites: job vacancy listing sites and employment agencies. Employment agencies act as 'middlemen' between you and the recruiter. Some recruitment sites are a combination of both job vacancy listings and employment agencies.

Why Use an Online Recruitment Site?

The simple answer to this question is: 'To improve your chances of finding the right job'. The way job sites can do this relates to the unique qualities of the Internet itself. Using the power of the Internet, job listing services and recruitment agencies can reach more employers and job-seekers than they can offline. As a result job and candidate databases on some of the larger sites have tens of thousands of entries.

However, although the obvious incentive for using these sites is to look through these vast databases, job sites and recruitment sites are not limited to this one single function. In fact, there are a number of different purposes to which job sites can be put. Here are some of the reasons why you might decide to use job sites and online recruitment agencies:

♦ *To search for vacancies.* The main reason most job-hunters use these sites is to search through a database of job listings. As some sites enable employers to post their job advertisements for free, online databases tend to be a lot more comprehensive than their offline counterparts. For instance, when we paid a visit to the UK version of the Monster Web site (*www.monster.co.uk*) we could search 15,164 UK jobs, more than 26,000 European jobs and over 440,000 global jobs.

♦ *To post your CV.* Most of the major recruitment sites enable you to post your CV online for employers to have a look at. The way this works varies from site to site. For instance, some sites allow you to post your CV as it is onto a candidate database, while others require you to tailor the CV to their own specifications.

♦ *To seek advice.* Many job and recruitment sites offer useful information and advice for people seeking employment. Again, the content and quality of this advice varies greatly between sites. Some provide useful information on how to put together your CV and covering letter, while others provide significant facts about certain industries or the job market as a whole.

♦ *To assess your abilities.* Some recruitment sites (such as Monster.com and Reed.co.uk to name but two) provide online self-assessment tests and questionnaires.

♦ *To network.* The fact that many recruitment sites include discussion forums means that you can make contact both with other job-seekers and employers.

Visiting Recruitment Sites

Most job-seekers view recruitment sites as places where they can browse through a directory of job vacancies and maybe submit their CV if they feel any vacancies are relevant. However, most of the major recruitment sites are much more than just 'job shops'. They are often a very useful source of information and advice on the job market as a whole.

Recruitment sites often feature useful articles on subjects such as 'How to Write the Perfect CV' or 'How to Handle Tough Interview Questions', and they often provide news items relating to specific industry sectors. In addition, many of the larger recruitment sites host discussion forums which enable you to ask fellow job-hunters, employers and employment experts for advice on areas you are having difficulty with.

One of the best recruitment sites for research information is

Reed.co.uk. This site offers job-seekers the chance to receive tailored information in its 'Career Streams' section. This information ranges from specialised career advice to the latest industry news. Career Streams also features a list of links and events relating to each industry.

Some sites have gone even further to provide candidates with useful information. For instance, in 2000, the graduate careers site Gradunet (*www.gradunet.co.uk*) launched a series of online career fairs, giving graduates the opportunity to meet employers via an Internet chat room.

However, even those recruitment sites which offer little more than a database of vacancies can prove to be valuable sources of information. By browsing through different vacancies, and by looking at what each employer's specific requirements are, you will be able to get a more informed picture of what your immediate career goals can and should be.

Below are some of the best recruitment sites for research purposes:

Go Job Site
www.gojobsite.co.uk

At Go Job Site job-seekers are provided with general careers advice alongside industry specific news relating to their area of interest.

Job Search
www.jobsearch.co.uk

Job Search offers useful free advice on putting together CVs and filling in application forms. As the site also has a database of over 10,000 vacancies it is a good place to research what employers are looking for and what sort of salary you can expect to earn.

Monster
www.monster.co.uk

As well as an enormous vacancy database, Monster also features a useful discussion forum.

Reed
www.reed.co.uk

As mentioned above, Reed.co.uk's 'Career Streams' section is a valuable source of information for the online job hunter.

As you might expect, the services offered by recruitment sites vary considerably. The recruitment site (or sites) you eventually opt for will depend on your own specific requirements and the type of job you are after. An obvious first port of call should be one of the larger higher-profile sites as they tend to offer the wider range of services. For instance, several of the major recruitment sites, including Monster.co.uk, Reed.co.uk, Stepstone.co.uk and Workthing.com (owned by the Guardian Media Group), offer facilities that allow you to register with them and then have vacancies which meet your requirements sent to you via e-mail as soon as they come in.

Although it may seem tempting to post your details to as many recruitment sites as possible, this is not a realistic option. This approach will lead to a severe case of 'information overload' as you will be bombarded with irrelevant vacancy details.

In fact, there will only be a few sites which can cater for your specific requirements. While you can search through the job databases with little concern, you therefore need to think very carefully about which sites you decide to submit your details to.

Here are some factors which should influence your decision:

♦ *The number of vacancies.* Sites with a large number of vacancies may offer a greater choice.
♦ *The relevance of the vacancies.* Some recruitment sites may *seem* to have a lot of jobs on offer but when it comes down to it very few may match your area of interest or expertise. You may find that some of the smaller, more specialised sites have more vacancies suited to your requirements.
♦ *Added value services.* Some job sites offer a range of additional services, such as career counselling.
♦ *Online opinion.* Checking out what other people think of a particular services before submitting your details is always a good idea. Ciao (*www.ciao.com*) and Epinions

(*www.epinions.com*) can both help you search for impartial comments and information posted by other job-seekers.

♦ *Search the site.* Although it may seem obvious, many people submit their details before checking out exactly what the site has to offer. It is only by searching through the vacancy database (and other relevant areas) that you will know if the site is for you.

The other reason to be careful when posting your CV details on the Internet is that, as well as potential employers, your present employer (if you have one) can also see it if they use that particular site.

Avoiding Rogue Sites

The fact that the Internet is such a convenient job-hunting tool means that thousands of recruitment sites have spring up over the last few years. Although many of these sites contain essential information and other useful services, many more may lead you in the wrong direction entirely.

The Internet has lowered the barriers of entry for those wishing to set up a recruitment business. As a result many companies have been set up which do not adhere to any recognised code of conduct.

The Association of Graduate Careers Advisory Services (AGCAS) is just one of the many organisations which has drawn attention to the threat posed by cowboy online recruitment sites. One of the main risks job-hunters face is that of sending CVs to their present employers because of the growing trade in personal details. Even if this does not happen, the more sloppy recruitment sites could pass your details around hundreds of organisations that you have no interest in working for. Caution is therefore necessary when approaching sites that offer to put your CV on the net, in order to make sure your details will only be received by relevant employers. You should also check exactly *how* your CV will be presented.

Here are some guidelines for approaching recruitment sites:

♦ *Don't pay for services.* Most professional careers and recruitment sites do not require any payment upfront for their services. If you do come across sites asking for money in return for quality advice and easy access to relevant jobs be very wary. According to Richard Nelson Bolles, author of the job-hunting classic *What Color is Your Parachute?*, 'The two warning bells to always listen for are: did they mention money (yours), and did they mention a check or credit card (yours)?' (see Further Reading).

◆ *Check for third-party approval.* Reputable recruitment sites tend to have the backing of a recognised, authoritative body such as AGCAS or the Association of Graduate Recruiters.

◆ *Go for personalised services.* The degree of personalisation offered by recruitment sites varies widely. It is important to use sites which avoid the scattergun, 'one-size-fits-all' approach to job-searching. Although form-filling can be a chore, the more information a recruitment site requires from you, the more likely it is that they will be able to 'matchmake' your skills and experience with a suitable vacancy.

◆ *Concentrate on content.* As AGCAS advise, 'Wacky design isn't everything – it's the expertise and advice behind the content that counts. OK, we all like sites that are quick, easy and fun, but don't forget that you are making introductions that could affect the rest of your life.'

◆ *Check if vacancies exist.* Unfortunately some recruitment agencies contain vacancies which do not exist. Although it is rare to find a site which deliberately misleads visitors by inventing vacancies (this is not unheard of, however), many sites contain out-of-date vacancies which have not been deleted from the database.

Providing the Right Information

In order to get the most out of a recruitment site you will need to submit information about yourself. At least, you will have to provide your name, e-mail address and the industry in which you are interested. Often, you will also be required to submit your CV for inclusion in a site's candidate database.

Providing personal information helps the recruitment site to assess the type of work you are looking for, and also enables any employers who use the site to see what you have to offer.

However, there are a few questions to ask before you decide to give any information away:

◆ *Will the information be passed on to other companies?* Sites can make a lot of money from selling lists of e-mail addresses to other companies. They can make even more money if they have detailed personal information on you. Sites are obliged to tell you if they plan to use your information in this way. Make sure that you never agree to this. Not only is it disrespectful of your privacy, but it also means you will be bombarded with 'spam' (junk) e-mails.

◆ *Will I be sent promotional material from the recruitment site?* Some recruitment sites automatically place your e-mail address on their mailing list unless you specifically tell them not to. While you may want to hear about the latest jobs in a certain industry, it is unlikely that you will want to be told how great the recruitment site is seven times a week.

◆ *Who will be able to access my information?* You will need to know who will access the information you provide. Some of the less scrupulous sites send CVs to employers who haven't even asked to see them. This not only gives a bad impression of the recruitment site, but of the candidate as well. Also, you want to make sure that your present employer will not be able to access the information – especially if they don't know you are seeking new employment! The more reputable recruitment agencies only contact an employer with your details if they have sought your permission first. However, even reputable agencies may share their database with other sites, so you need to check which other recruitment sites may use your details.

The Main Recruitment Sites

There are two main types of recruitment site: general sites (catch-all sites aimed at all job-hunters) and specialised sites (based around specific industries).

Most sites are free to use for people searching for a job. Most sites allow you to run your own searches direct from their home page, although some require you to register with them before you can proceed further. You can post your CV on some sites and it is then e-mailed to the employment agency or put on display for employers to browse through. Some sites will notify you by e-mail when jobs that match your search criteria are posted by employers, which saves you from having to revisit their site.

Although most of the recruitment sites mentioned here can help job-seekers maximise their chances of finding the right job, it is important not to be seduced by some of the job sites' more extravagant claims. Simply posting your CV online at one of these sites will not guarantee a suitable job. There are literally thousands of job-seekers who have posted their CVs onto sites with little or no success whatsoever.

This does not mean that these people are incapable of getting a job. What it does indicate, however, is that the recruitment process at whichever sites they use is not perfectly suited to their requirements.

While recruitment Web sites can play a central role in your online job hunting activity, they should therefore never be your only hope.

General Recruitment Sites

Apply4it.co.uk
www.apply4it.co.uk

Apply4it offers general services for Berkshire, Thames Valley, and the South East provided by local independent recruitment agencies.

Go Job Site
www.gojobsite.co.uk

Go Job Site is one of the largest UK recruitment sites with a database of over 200,000 jobs around Europe. Every Go Job Site candidate is provided with their own 'My Go Job Site' Web page that delivers a service tailored specifically for the industry sector.

Candidates can apply for advertised vacancies online and are asked to provide a CV and covering letter.

Applications are recorded in the candidate's 'My Go Job

Site' so contact with the recruiter can be monitored and documented throughout the recruitment process.

As well as applying for specific positions, job-seekers can also ask Go Job Site to distribute their CV details to hundreds of relevant recruitment agencies simultaneously. According to Go Job Site, 'This outstanding service provides job-hunters with instant exposure at a level that is virtually unachievable using traditional recruitment methods'.

Go Job Site provides an overnight e-mail service enabling job-seekers to receive the latest news on relevant vacancies. Candidates are also offered general careers advice to help them prepare thoroughly for the job-seeking process, as well as industry specific news relating to their area of interest.

Go Job Site has consistently been voted number one recruitment site in independent Internet recruitment surveys (RMS Media tech, Riley/Recruitment, MMXI Europe). It has an intuitive uncluttered site design, rapid job-searching, extensive careers advice and high security for your CV. It is also easy to apply for jobs by cutting and pasting your CV and covering letter into the fields provided. With more than 50,000 jobs on the site every day across 30 industry sectors and with no old jobs on the site it is the leading recruitment site in the UK.

Job Search
www.jobsearch.co.uk

This general recruitment site boasts over 10,000 vacancies and enables you to submit your CV onto its candidate database for free. The Job Search Site also provides useful advice on writing a CV and preparing for an interview. To submit your CV to Job Search you simply complete an online form and when you have pressed the submit button your entry will be placed online immediately.

Monster
www.monster.co.uk

The UK version of the site which became famous as 'the monster board' has one of the largest job indexes on the Web. The vast job database includes jobs from about 50 countries around the world. Furthermore, monster.co.uk also offers what has to be the best job discussion forum on the Web, making it the Godzilla of recruitment sites. Although, monster.co.uk is more of a job posting board than anything else, it does offer candidate–employer matchmaking services.

Recruit Online
www.recruit-online.com

Recruit Online has a comprehensive directory of UK recruitment agencies which are searchable by industry sector.

Reed
www.reed.co.uk

Reed.co.uk is one of the big guns in the world of online recruitment. One of the main features of the site is the Job Sleuth service. Job Sleuth automatically sends candidates vacancy information matching their requirements to the candidate's e-mail address or via text message to their mobile phone.

However, this is by no means the only service Reed.co.uk offers. With over 1,600 specialist consultants and over 40,000 vacancies at any time, Reed.co.uk takes a very active role in matching job-hunters with the right employers.

Many of the vacancies are placed on the site by Reed.co.uk consultants acting as agents for employers. Any vacancies not handled by Reed.co.uk are clearly identified as such, and your application would be sent directly to the employer. If you are applying for a job through Reed.co.uk, then your application details will go to the Reed recruitment consultant who handles that specific employer. If the consultant feels that you are up to the job they will forward your application to the employer and then contact you to tell you what the next step involves.

The career streams Reed caters for include 'accountancy, finance, banking and insurance', 'administration, PA, secretarial and customer service', 'catering, hospitality, retail and leisure', 'executive and professional', 'graduate opportunities', 'health, care and education', 'HR, recruitment and training', 'IT, new media and telecoms', 'PR, media and creative', 'sales and marketing', and 'technical, engineering and scientific'.

The site therefore enables candidates to concentrate solely on their particular career area. Reed.co.uk also offers a wide range of tailored information in its 'Career Streams' section, from the latest industry news to specialised career advice, as well as links and events of interest to job-seekers in that industry.

The site also features a regional salary calculator enabling you to 'see whether the grass really is greener on the other side' and providing an instant guide to comparative salaries throughout the UK. Based on your current salary and average salaries nationwide, the calculator will tell you what you could expect to earn anywhere else in the country.

One of the reasons why Reed.co.uk can boast such a large number of vacancies is because it lets recruitment agencies place as many advertisements as they want free of charge.

Step Stone
www.stepstone.com

Billing itself as 'Europe's career portal', Step Stone is a general recruitment site containing one of the largest employment databases on the Internet (with over 100,000 job vacancies). Subject areas include: 'agriculture, environment and marine', 'business administration and management', 'education and training', 'civil engineering and construction', 'engineering', 'financial services', 'hairdressing and beauty', 'marketing sales and customer service', 'medical, health and veterinary' and 'politics, economics and law'.

Specialised recruitment sites:

Boldly – Go
www.boldy-go.com

Referring to itself as a 'relationship broker' (whatever that means), the Boldly–Go site provides staff for e-businesses at the embryonic stage of development. They type of jobs on offer are therefore in accord with the requirements of dot.com companies (financial, technological, operational, human resources, content provision, etc.). The site is particularly useful for those seeking top-level positions.

Brook Street
www.brookstreet.co.uk

Brook Street specialises in secretarial, office and light industrial recruitment. Permanent, temporary and contract positions are all available at this site.

Computer People
www.computerpeople.co.uk

Set up in 1972, Computer People now claims to be the UK's most successful recruitment consultancy specialising in the provision of skilled IT personnel. The company does indeed have a long-standing reputation for successfully recruiting experienced IT professionals on both a permanent and a contract basis. Computer People now has an excellent new media section with a vast choice of vacancies.

Elan Computing
www.elancomputing.com

Elan Computing is another leading IT recruiter and now operates as the IT arm of the Manpower Group. Elan places IT professionals in over 900 companies around the globe and has a graduate recruitment section.

Golden Square
www.goldensquare.com

UK and European recruitment consultants specialising in IT, secretarial, legal, design and new media jobs.

Graduate Base
www.graduatebase.com

Graduate Base is one of the leading UK graduate recruitment sites. The site offers advice and career planning as well as recruitment services for UK student and graduates.

Major Players
www.majorplayers.co.uk

> Major Players is a recruitment site specialising in marketing and new media jobs. As with most of the other recruitment sites it enables you to submit your CV for free by filling in an online form. An e-mail alert service is also provided, which sends candidates information on the latest marketing and new media jobs direct to their inboxes. Major Players covers permanent, temporary and freelance jobs and has a graduate section.

Pelican Consultants
www.pelican-consultants.com

> This site specialises in new media recruitment and has a wide range of up-to-date commercial and development vacancies on the industry.

Source That Job
www.sourcethatjob.com

> The Source That Job site specialises in media jobs relating to career areas such as advertising, marketing and public relations.
>
> The job categories on offer include administration, design, media sales, office management, purchasing, advertising, creative, design management, direct marketing, IT, personnel, sales, new media, human resources and public relations.

Case studies

Trudy finds a rogue recruitment site

Trudy decides to search some recruitment sites to look for job vacancies in Belfast. She searches for recruitment sites at a large search engine and is provided with a long list of recruitment company Web sites. Trudy clicks on one site which looks interesting because it promises that it will be able to find her a suitable job in the first month of registering.

When Trudy logs onto the site she is asked to fill in an application form. Trudy completes the application form but at the end of the form there are payment details and no privacy statement. There had been no mention of payment on the home page and therefore Trudy is wary of the site and does not pay for the recruitment company services.

Philip uses a specialist recruitment company

Philip decides to use the services of a specialist accountancy recruitment agency. He uses the UK version of About.com to locate relevant accountancy agencies in London. He links to the 'Accountancy Jobs' section on the About.com recruitment homepage which provides him with a list of accountancy agencies. He chooses Hays Accountancy Personnel (*www.hays-ap.com*) because he knows it is a large reputable company and believes it will have a huge database of relevant jobs.

Philip uses the 'Find that Job' section of the site to try to locate a relevant job. From this page he links to the accountancy and finance section and then to the 'Jobs Available in London' section. There are 14 relevant openings advertised on the site with two of the jobs looking very interesting to him: one at Barclays and the other at Legal & General. Philip cuts and pastes the information to a folder on his hard drive.

The Hays Web site also has a 'top companies' section which includes an overview of the mobile communications company Orange which provides further information on accountancy jobs at the company.

Checklist

To make the most of online recruitment sites remember to:

- ◆ *Find the right site for you.* Look for the number of relevant vacancies before you sign in.
- ◆ *Use the added extras.* Use the job e-mails, recruitment articles, industry links and discussion groups to your advantage.
- ◆ *Decide on agency or database.* Decide if you want to use an agency site or job database site.
- ◆ *Avoid rogue sites.* Avoid rogue sites that may be promoting vacancies that do not exist.
- ◆ *Go for personalised services.*

CHAPTER 5

Networking Online

There are millions of Web sites that allow some kind of discussion online. These range from small-scale industry-specific forums to general job-seeking communities on large commercial sites. To understand the benefits of online interaction, it is first important to acknowledge the different ways people can communicate with each other on the Internet.

If you communicate with people online in real time this is known as 'synchronous' communication, whereas if you leave messages for people to read and reply to later this is known as 'asynchronous' communication. Synchronous communication can be found in different forms, including online chatrooms, Internet-based chat services such as Internet Relay Chat (IRC), specialised chat services (for example *www.mirabilis.com*) and video conferencing. The main way to communicate asynchronously is via e-mail but you can also use Web-based bulletin boards and newsgroups (often known as discussion groups).

After e-mail, newsgroups are the most common communication tool online and as such are the main focus of this chapter.

What are Newsgroups?

There are two types of newsgroup: one is based on e-mail software called list servers (such as Outlook Express) and the other is based on the Web. People who are interested in similar subjects discuss ideas and theories in these groups. They work very simply with one person posting a message or question and then other group members replying. The reply posting is called a thread.

The main newsgroup system is called Usenet and there are tens of thousands of Usenet newsgroups dedicated to every subject imaginable. As the topic range is so vast it should not be too difficult for you to find a Usenet discussion which is relevant to your job-hunt. The Usenet provider (normally your ISP) has a database of articles which is updated continuously. If you are a member of a group articles are dispatched to you as soon as they are received.

Newsgroups on the Web

Newsgroups can be accessed online via the following Web sites:

Domeus
www.ecircle-uk.com

Domeus includes discussion forums, mailing lists and e-mail groups. With Domeus you can post and read messages straight from your e-mail. You do not have to subscribe to the group to send messages. You only need to subscribe if you want to receive all messages. You can simply click on the messages online or send an e-mail to subscribe.

Egroups
www.egroups.co.uk

Egroups is a free e-mail group service that allows you to easily join e-mail groups. The main benefits of e-groups include: a customised 'My Groups Page' where you can access all the groups you have joined; a choice of how to view your messages (you can receive individual messages via e-mail or receive a daily digest via e-mail or view them online); a strict anti-spam policy; and a 24-hour customer support team.

Google
http://groups.google.com

Google has an archive of over 500 million messages and it provides very high-speed access. This service remains the most popular of its kind on the Internet.

Liszt
www.liszt.com

Liszt has a database of 30,000 Usenet newsgroups, 80,000 mailing lists and 25,000 IRC Chat Channels.

Smartgroups
www.smartgroups.com

Smartgroups is a free service for group communication. The site includes a wide range of job newsgroups. Here are three of them:

- *IT Jobs in London* – a group set up to introduce individuals to new jobs in the IT sector in London;
- *Club DJ* – information on club culture jobs;
- *Cruise Ship* – Information on jobs in the cruise ship industry.

Tile
www.tile.net

Tile provides links to newsgroups and mailing lists.

Topica
www.topica.com

Topica is a free Internet service that allows you to find, manage and participate in e-mail lists. It provides easy access for the average Internet user, has nearly one million new subscriptions per month and delivers nearly 300 million e-mail messages monthly.

Topica provides e-mail newsletters, tips and discussions. In the 'Useful tips in handy e-mails' section there is a 'Job of the Day' feature which is likely to be of value to Internet job-hunters. Also the site provides a 'My Topica page' which helps you keep track of what you have subscribed to.

Yahoo!
www.yahoo.co.uk

To join a Yahoo! club you simply search through the categories until you find one of interest, you then click on that club name and click to join.

Other searchable Usenet archives include:

- **Easy Usenet**   *www.easyusenet.com*
- **Internet Public Library**   *www.ipl.org*

- ◆ News One   *www.newsone.net*
- ◆ News Ranger   *newsranger.com*
- ◆ News Walk   *www.nooz.net*
- ◆ News2Web   *www.news2web.com*
- ◆ Usenet4Free   *www.usenet4free.com*

You can also find specialised newsgroup web sites described below:

Recruitment newsgroup web sites

A handful of the online recruitment sites also include discussion areas. Monster (*www.monster.co.uk*) is the most popular with eleven different forums which include: campus, local government, international, legal, power and utilities, healthcare, technology, learning and training, teenzone and call centre. The site allows users to share their experiences with other people in their field.

Another popular online recruitment site which includes newsgroups is Career Mag (*www.careermag.com*). The message board is moderated here and the discussions on employment include: job search issues, work place issues, internships, campus, working from home and a career coach section.

Industry newsgroup web sites

Industry-specific discussion sites are available. One such example is Chinwag (*www.chinwag.com*), a directory of newsgroups and mailing lists focused on marketing and technical services.

Local areas

If you are searching for a job in a specific area it may be useful to locate some local newsgroups. The newsgroup users may have local vacancy information. The best way to locate local newsgroups would be to use one of the large search engine sites. If you enter relevant keywords into the search engine and also include the words 'newsgroup' or 'discussion group' your return results will include newsgroups that use your keywords frequently. This may be a good place to start your newsgroup searching.

E-mail Newsgroups

So far we have covered newsgroups which can be used on a Web interface, which makes it easy for the first-time user to access and get to grips with. However, if you plan to use newsgroups frequently it is worth taking the time to understand the other main system which is via e-mail. This will save you time and money in the long term because with e-mail newsgroups you download the Usenet messages on to your hard drive for you to reply to later (less online time is therefore required).

Here are the steps you should take to access newsgroups via e-mail:

1 *Open your e-mail software.* You can use e-mail to send your message but there is also software that is dedicated to sending and receiving Usenet mailing such as Forte Free Agent (*www.forteinc.com*) and Micro Planet Gravity (*www.totalshareware.com*) which have more features than your standard e-mail programs such as Outlook Express.

2. *Locate the newsgroup folder.* Your ISP has probably loaded the newsgroup files for you and they should be among your e-mail folders. The site title should incorporate the name of your ISP, for example 'ntlworld-news'. The newsgroups are displayed in a long list (there are thousands of them) with normally a one sentence description.

3. *If there is a problem contact your ISP.* If you do not have a file here contact your ISP to find out how to set it up by hand.

4. *Open the Newsgroup file.* The newsgroup file contains the names of all of the newsgroups known to your ISP. Your Web browser uses newsfeeds (which are provided by your ISP) to access all the newsgroup information and downloads it to your computer. If you have correctly set the newsreader and you have tried to contact a newsgroup with little success that is probably because your ISP does not subscribe to it.

5. *Search the newsgroups*

You are now ready to search the newsgroups. (A complete list

of all UK newsgroup listings can be found at
www.usenet.org.uk/newsgroups.html and assistance for Usenet
readers in the UK can be found at the Usenet UK organisation
at *www.usenet.org.uk.*)

Searching the Newsgroups

Searching newsgroups via a web-based interface is simple,
especially if you have managed search engine techniques, as the
procedure is exactly the same (see the next chapter for further
information). They all include search boxes on their home
pages into which you should type your keywords into the site
to return a list of newsgroups that match your search.

Some newsgroup sites provide lists of all the Usenet
messages that contain your keyword query. For example, when
the keyword 'jobs' was typed into Google the return results
were two newsgroup sites which included comp.jobs.computer
and can.jobs and 980,000 relevant Usenet messages. When the
keywords were narrowed slightly to 'uk jobs' the results were
three newsgroup sites (*uk.jobs.offered, uk.jobs.contract* and
uk.jobs.d) and 318,000 relevant Usenet messages. Google also
gives you the opportunity to search only specific newsgroups.
In a search for 'design jobs' in the uk.jobs.d newsgroup 43
messages were returned. Although 10 per cent of the 43
messages were not relevant at least 20 per cent were offering
jobs in the design field and most offered some advice.

Searching e-mail newsgroups is just as simple but may take
a little more getting used to. If you open up your newsgroup
file a list of newsgroups that your ISP subscribes to will appear
with a one-sentence description next to them. This will be a
long list because there are thousands of newsgroups available.
Although in theory you can scroll down this list and choose
suitable newsgroups by hand, this would be a very time-
consuming process.

Fortunately, there is also a search option in your newsreader
which allows you to search all of the newsgroups quickly.
Simply type in your key words and the reader will supply you
with a list of results that match your query. To access the list
click on it and your reader will download all the messages to
your browser from the ISP.

Newsgroup Names

Newsgroup domain names are similar to Web site domain names and they explain a lot about the newsgroup. Newsgroup domain names include a main newsgroup heading such as:

alt	alternative
sci	science
com	computing
uk	united kingdom
rec	recreation
biz	business
talk	debate orientated
misc	miscellaneous

Comprehensive listings of Usenet headings can be found at The Daily News (*www.newsguy.com*).

The main newsgroups then have subcategories followed by sub-subcategories. For example, with the newsgroup 'uk.jobs.d': 'uk' is the heading, 'jobs' is the subcategory and 'd' is the sub-subcategory. From this information the reader can derive that the newsgroup is UK focused on and discusses (the 'd' stands for discussion) jobs.

There are specialised newsgroups and mailing lists that cover Internet job searching which you may find useful. They include:

uk.jobs.d	Discussion of jobs-related issues
uk.jobs.offered	Situations vacant. No discussion
uk.jobs.wanted	Situations wanted. No discussion
uk.jobs.contract	Contract positions wanted/offered
uk.jobs.fortyplus	Jobs for the over forties

If you are trying to find a job in a specific job sector there are a number of newsgroups that cover market sectors. These newsgroups are particularly useful for research on specific companies. They include:

uk.business.accountancy	UK accounting, auditing and taxation
uk.business.agriculture	Agriculture industry in UK
uk.business.payroll	Payroll practices, procedure and legislation
uk.business.worker	Teleworkers and their employers

Once a relevant discussion list has been located to receive the message frequently you will need to subscribe to the list. This normally involves completing a registration form or, in the case of an e-mail newsgroup, sending an e-mail to the server's address. You must subscribe to a Usenet newsgroup but this should not involve any form of payment.

Learning to 'Lurk'

Now you have located and registered for the newsgroups that are relevant, you are nearly ready to start posting messages. But before you start participating in newsgroups you should learn to 'lurk'. Lurking is reading the messages that are posted in a discussion without taking an active part. The main reason you should lurk is to start to understand the dynamics of the group before you start to interact. By lurking you can estimate what questions will and will not be answered and who you should direct your questions at. You will also be able to make sure that the group is right for your wants and needs.

All newsgroups are archived so past responses can be searched for and read. You may find that your question has already been answered by someone months ago. One of the biggest mistakes you could make is to rush headlong into a newsgroup bombarding it with lots of questions. Remember to check out recent and past messages because perhaps your question has already been answered.

Also, look at when the last message was posted onto the site before actually posting anything yourself. If no one has used the board in the last two weeks then it may be a waste of time posting because it is unlikely that you will receive a reply. The busiest newsgroups are normally those found at the big Web sites such as Yahoo!

Some discussion lists may be unmoderated. In unmoderated lists no one is there to check the content of each message. In moderated lists, on the other hand, all messages are checked and the moderator can edit or delete messages at his or her discretion. It is preferable for the purpose of job-hunting to use a moderated list.

Newsgroup 'Netiquette'

As with e-mail, in newsgroups you run the risk of being
'flamed'. A flame is a message sent to someone who has
annoyed or irritated the sender and is the ultimate rebuke. If
you follow the advice below you are unlikely to suffer this
humiliation:

♦ *Be relevant.* Keep to the subject and only post messages to
relevant newsgroups.

♦ *Keep it short.* Keep the question or message short. If your
questions are longwinded and don't get to the point quickly
and clearly this may result in no one reading them.

♦ *Be polite.* Be polite and friendly at all times.

♦ *Lurk.* Get to know the group before you start posting.

♦ *Don't cross post.* Try and use one newsgroup at a time. You
run the risk of getting 'flamed' if you send the same
message/question to multiple newsgroups.

♦ *Don't use HTML.* Do not use HTML. Although some
newsreaders accept HTML formats some do not and
therefore certain newsgroup members will not be able to
read the e-mail. HTML postings also take up extra
bandwidth when they are being downloaded onto recipient's
computers.

♦ *Spam.* Do not send spam. That is to say do not send
irrelevant messages selling yourself or your services. As ISPs
are continuously filtering out spam you may run the risk of
being discarded by the ISP as well as the newsgroup.

♦ *Don't over quote.* If you are replying to a message only copy
the information that is relevant. People do not appreciate
receiving large messages.

♦ *Read the FAQs.* There will normally be an FAQ or
'frequently asked questions' list on the newsgroup. The FAQ
list answers any basic questions which you may have. This is
normally posted to the group once a month at the least.
Read the list before you start posting messages to the group
– it may stop you repeating a question which has been
asked one hundred times before.

♦ *No shouting.* Do not SHOUT by using capital letters all the
time.

♦ *Look for moderated groups.* Moderated newsgroups have a

person responsible for them and therefore they include less spam messages and the messages that are included are normally of a higher quality. Please note that because each message is read by the moderator before they are issued to the group it may take a while for your message to be posted, and you may be asked to rewrite it if the moderator finds the content unsuitable.

◆ *For your own safety:*
  – Don't give your e-mail address to anyone.
  – Don't give your full name to anyone.
  – And most importantly don't disclose your address or telephone number.

Asking the Right Questions

Now you are ready to send messages you must be careful how you phrase your questions and queries. Don't ask unnecessary questions unless you are prepared for some angry replies. Newsgroups are pretty informal places as you will soon realise after using them for a while so try and use informal language. It is always good to give a brief overview of your situation (especially if you are new to the group). Here are three different newsgroup messages with their thread replies.

Newsgroup message 1

I've been currently working in local government for the past 2 yrs. Since starting this role, I have become very interested in the IT side of things. I quite often help colleagues out with Microsoft problems and general PC problems. I have been told I have missed my vocation in life and should work with computers – now I don't know which way to go!

A career in computing does appeal to me, but I am not sure how to go about getting into this field. I also find that I am very creative (working with Paint Shop Pro etc.) and enjoy building my own Web sites, without HTML I add, but this is also something I would like to get into!

Is there any hope for me...?

Thread reply 1

Hi, read your message on technology message board. My advice is to go for it and do it now before it is too late. I am 38 years old and just starting out in the IT industry, well not actually starting out, more like on the threshold. A year ago I was in a dead-end job in the food industry. For years since leaving the armed forces I wanted to either go to college or try distance learning. Finance held me back and supporting a family. When redundancy reared its head at work, I volunteered and took the money. I think I have made a solid investment by going into distance learning studying applications programming with Computeach International. Their ads appear in most local and national press. I was lucky enough to find a job which allowed me to work and study at the same time. Work by day, study evenings. There are also some great e-commerce sites which, through government funding, allow you to use the Internet for studying different application systems and program suites for further development at low cost. I am not suggesting you pack in your job, only consider distance learning, night school or using government funded ILA's to study at home over the Internet.

Try these sites for further information:

www.computeach.co.uk

Rather pricey but worth it if you can afford it and have the commitment.

www.ilearnto.co.uk

An online learning service, or also

www.learndirect.co.uk or is it .com can't remember.

Let me know how you progress.

Newsgroup message 2

My name is Paulo and I'm a final year Law & Management student. Even though my course is concentrating heavily on the law subjects (90% of the 4 years units are law), my main worry and the reason I write for advice is my future prospects of a career. I'd like to work in companies' legal depts and preferably in shipping companies' legal depts but from some browsing I did in the job section most ads ask for qualified lawyer/ solicitor. So would my combined law & management degree be sufficient or would I have to study for a further 2 years in order to gain a strictly law degree? As I reach the end of my course in May I have to start planning what to do next year and in the near future. Is a Masters degree also an advantage in legal positions? It would be a tremendous help if someone could answer my e-mail. Thank you very much.

A troubled/confused near graduate.

Thread reply 2

It is probably better that you have a split degree. You need to do the LPC next – legal professional qualification and then articles: some firms help with the cost of articles as they see you as investing in their future. LPC fees are £5,000.

Look up a reference book in a library concerning law firms, such as Legal 500, the Bar Directory and others, and they will tell you who are doing 'shipping'. Ince & Co, near Tower Bridge, London who are shipping, air. You might like to see if they have a Web site – try *www.barcouncil.org(.uk)* for links to lawyers or *www.lawzone.co.uk* (or .com) as another useful reference Web site – there are loads of legal Web sites now. *www.scl.org.uk* is another.

Newsgroup message 3

I'm a professional freelance writer in search of paying assignments. I wrote for printing and publishing trade magazines for five years, and then followed that up with almost a decade of writing about medical topics. I'm trying to 'branch out'. Are there any good Web sites out there listing paying freelance writing gigs?

Thread reply 3

There are:

http://freelancewrite.about.com/careers/freelancewrite/bljobpage.html
http://ajr.newslink.org
http://www.sunoasis.com/freelance.html
http://www.mediabistro.com/joblistings/
http://www.newsjobs.net

To name a few. Note that the AJR site lets you set up e-mail notification of jobs fitting your criteria. Newsjobs is a master list of more than 100 writing job Web sites. The About.com site lets you sign up for a worthwhile newsletter with assignment leads. A few other free e-mail newsletters are worth getting as well, including:

www.writing4money.com

Check these sites and their links, sign up for e-mail bulletins and newsletters, do searches for 'freelance writing' and monitor this newsgroup. And let us know how it goes.

Best
Ruth

As you can see from the above, newsgroups can provide valuable information and help if the question is right.

Submitting Newsgroup Postings

Here are some guidelines for sending your newsgroup messages:

◆ *Stick to plain text.* Newsgroup postings can be made in plain text format or HTML. Stick to plain text format because some computers do not support HTML and it also takes longer to download and send HTML files.

◆ *Use a free online e-mail address.* Also, when sending a newsgroup message it may be worth using a different e-mail address because newsgroups often receive mountains of spam e-mail. A good idea would be to use one of the free online services such as Hotmail (*www.hotmail.com*) or Yahoo! (*www.yahoo.com*). Then if you receive too much spam you can quite easily close the account and open a new one.

◆ *Don't send attachments.* You can send attachments to newsgroups but if you are fairly new to newsgroups it is best not to.

♦ *Be patient.* When you post your message it is sent to your ISP's news server which then distributes the message to everyone in the newsgroup (this can take hours and sometimes even days to complete if the newsgroup has a lot of members). Postings therefore normally take a few days to appear.

Getting to Know the Advisors

Once you have been contributing to the group for a while you will start to realise that out of 1,000 members only 50 contribute regularly and of these only 1–10 are group advisors. Group advisors are reliable and useful resources of information when you are searching for a job online. Their knowledge could help you immensely in your Internet job search.

It is sometimes easy to work out who the group advisors are as they are often mentioned as such in the discussions. Furthermore, certain members direct their discussion mail directly at them. It may take some detective work to locate the advisors but it will be beneficial in the long run because the advisors understand and have an in-depth knowledge of the newsgroup subject.

Other 'Cyber Societies' for Job-seekers

Although the focus of this chapter has been on online and e-mail discussion groups, there are many other cyber societies. These include the following:

Web sites

A lot of recruitment Web pages include bulletin boards where users can leave messages.

Mailing lists

Mailing lists are similar to e-mail newsgroups although they are normally one-way rather than two-way communication tools. These one-way messages are particularly useful if they have been produced by a company you would like to work for. A number of larger company sites include mailing lists which can be registered for at the site.

Mailing lists can be searched for at Liszt (*www.liszt.com*) and E-zine Central (*www.e-zinecentral.com*). E-zine Central is an American site which provides a quick and easy way to subscribe to hundreds of free quality e-mail newsletters and publications. Examples include the Cyber Times, a free information technology newsletter which claims to include 'hot IT jobs'.

A good example of a UK mailing list is UKNM-jobs. This mailing list is perfect if you are looking for a job in new media. As with all one-way mailing lists it is an announcement only list so you can only receive job vacancy information and not participate in a discussion.

Chat areas

Chat areas are live communication areas where people exchange messages (or chat) via text messages. Chat is less formal than newsgroups and due to its immediate nature it is rarely recorded anywhere. There are two main types of chat: Internet Relay Chat (IRC) and Web-based chat. If the chatroom you want to join is Web-based you will not need extra software because it is run by using Web browsers and online forms. Internet Relay Chat on the other hand requires software but this can be downloaded onto your computer for free. A guide can be found at a *www.ahandyguide.com*.

If you type a question or sentence into a chat area, people will be able to see it and reply to your query immediately. There are two disadvantages to chat areas. Firstly, there is a slight delay when you use them because the technology is not as advanced as it needs to be. Secondly, people who use chatrooms also use a lot of technical jargon. A good example of a job chatroom can be found by logging on to *uk.chat.yahoo.com/c/roomlist.html* and then clicking on Career Corner.

Members only areas

Some Internet Service Providers, such as AOL and

Compuserve, offer message boards but only if you have subscribed to their service. Private newsgroups have hosts to check all the messages.

Case studies

Philip uses e-mail newsgroups

Philip decides to find out more about the telecommunications industry in general and Orange in particular by talking to people in a newsgroup (he uses a newsgroup service via his e-mail system). He configures and locates his newsgroup easily and finds a relevant newsgroup via a keyword search. He types the words 'UK and telecom' which return the newsgroup entitled uk.telecommobile. Philip opens up the newsgroup and starts to read the messages. One of the first messages reads:

> At last there is a site dedicated to jobs in the cellular industry. *www.umstwork.com* has loads of jobs direct from recruiters and some agencies.

This looks appealing to Philip so he accesses the UMST work site and registers for their job alert system so jobs can be sent direct to his e-mail inbox.

Rajesh searches the Google newsgroup

Rajesh wants to find out more about special needs teaching and is interested in talking to other people in the profession who have followed a similar path to the one he intends to take. He decides to use a Web-based newsgroup and opts for Google (*http://groups.google.com*). He uses the search keywords 'special needs teaching UK' in the newsgroup search engine. The search returns one relevant newsgroup entitled 'uk.eduation.teachers' and 691 specific messages.

Rajesh looks at the first message which is headed 'Special Needs teaching advice needed'. The message is from someone in exactly the same position as himself who wants advice on training requirements. The reply posts claim that working in this field is very hard work but also very rewarding. A number of the reply posts advocate the Open University Diploma in Special Needs.

Checklist

A number of employers (especially in the technical sector) prefer to use newsgroups to post job vacancies or search for new employees, so mastering newsgroups is essential if you want to maximise the chances of securing your dream job. When using newsgroups you must adhere to the following advice:

◆ *Conduct a thorough newsgroup search.* Due to the sheer amount of newsgroups ensure you have searched thoroughly to find the right group for your job search.

◆ *Lurk before you post.* Before you start posting to newsgroups become a silent visitor for a while. You don't want to make a fool of yourself in your first posting.

◆ *Ask the right questions.* To receive the best responses you must ask the right questions. Be brief and to the point but give the reader enough information to work with.

◆ *Be a good newsgroup 'netizen'.* Follow the netiquette guidelines and you will be well on your way to being a respected member of the online community.

◆ *Use the Internet as a two-way communication tool.* The Internet is a two-way communication tool so use this to your advantage with newsgroups, chatrooms and bulletin boards.

◆ *Gather research via mailing lists.* Use mailing lists to help you simplify your job research.

CHAPTER 6

Using Search Engines in Your Job-hunt

T he World Wide Web is growing exponentially, and
    although no one knows the exact total it is estimated that
there are over one billion Web pages on the Web. Finding
your way around can be very confusing, but if used properly
search engines can help you find what you are looking for in
seconds.

Searching the Web can be a very useful, even essential, part
of the job-seeking process. Most of the larger company Web
sites include search engines so searching is almost inevitable
even if you avoid the main search sites. Knowing how to
conduct a targeted search is therefore a very useful skill to
learn. After all, if your search is too broad your results could be
in the thousands or if your search is too narrow there could be
too few results. Either way the searcher may miss out on the
job of their dreams. This chapter discusses search engines,
directories and the techniques that should be utilised to find
what you want quickly and painlessly.

Understanding Search Engines

Search engines have vast databases full of different Web pages.
The search engines use special search technology often referred
to as 'robots' to trawl the Web and store information onto their
databases and keep up-to-date. When you start a search the
search engine looks through it's database of Web pages to find
entries that match your query. Search engines provide an
enormous amount of information. In fact, some search engines
don't just search Web pages but also discussion groups, audio
files and picture files.

Search engines work in different ways and they all have their
own method of deciding which Web pages are most relevant to

your query. Certain search engines will only search the Web page title while others will search the whole of the document. Other Web sites rate pages on the number of links they contain – the theory being the more links the better the site. The more relevant the search engine deems the Web page the higher the result will appear in the return list. This is why you receive different results with different search engines.

After the engine completes its search it returns a list of site links (this normally takes less than 10 seconds). Each link allows you to click through to the highlighted Web site. The list of links include overviews of the Web sites (this may be just a list of keywords) which helps you decide if the Web site is worth clicking onto and viewing. The results are also ranked in order of best match.

Alongside the standard search engine sites there are other types of search sites including directories, specialised search engines and white pages. Although directories are often referred to as search engines, there is a difference. Search engines, as we have discovered, use robots to trawl the World Wide Web to find new or updated Web sites. Directories, on the other hand, rely on human beings to update their content. Directories often rate Web sites according to content and only the highest quality sites are included in their databases. This is especially useful for job seekers new to the Internet who do not want to waste time looking through lists of irrelevant Web pages. Directories are particularly good at researching a specific field such as Fashion because you can 'browse' by subject. Directories include categories such as jobs and then subcategories such as recruitment firms. The subcategories contain more subsections and so on. You must keep clicking down the subcategories to end up at the site you want.

Search engines, on the other hand, would just show a very long list of Web sites if you typed the word 'fashion'. However, search engines are excellent research tools if you know exactly what you are looking for. A lot of sites such as Yahoo! and Excite are essentially directories but with a search engine attached.

If you are searching for a specific company online a good option would be to look at a search Web site known as a 'white pages' site (see below). Specialised search engines will save you time because they focus on specific subjects. The results of your search are normally more targeted than the 'catch-all' search engines because specialised search engines do not use robots to search the Web, they use real people.

The Main Search Sites

The main search engines are normally well maintained and up-to-date. The most well-known search engines are as follows:

Alta Vista
www.altavista.com or *www.altavista.co.uk*

Alta Vista is one of the oldest and most popular of the major search engines. It is available in 25 languages and it also has a 'Breaking News' section. It's Advanced Search tutorials and Advanced Search Cheat Sheet help you to search the site. Alta Vista includes a list of the 'hot searches' which are the most frequently typed keywords. Significantly for job-seekers, Alta Vista includes a Web directory which has a careers section.

Excite
www.excite.com or *www.excite.co.uk*

Excite offers various choices for narrowing searches. You can choose to search the 'Web', 'news', 'photos' or 'products'. Excite also includes the Excite Channel which is a directory and has a jobs and careers section.

Go
www.go.com

This site offers a 'Power Search' facility which helps you refine your search. Go.com also offers the Go Express Search which 'combs the Web with the power of the top ten search engines'.

Google
www.google.com

Google is one of the largest and most popular search engines. Google's home page shows how many Web pages it will search. At the time of writing it was 1,346,966,000. Google also contains a Web directory which organises the most popular sites by topic.

GoTo
www.goto.com or www.goto.co.uk

As well as offering a simple search engine GoTo offers you the choice of browsing their most popular search categories.

HotBot
www.hotbot.com

HotBot has an advanced search option as well as a HotBot directory. In the HotBot directory the Jobs link can be found in the Business and Money section.

Looksmart
www.looksmart.com or www.looksmart.co.uk

Looksmart includes a basic keyword search box, as well as help and information on searching by category and keyword. According to the Looksmart homepage the search directory indexes 'quality sites, chosen by editors'. The Jobs link can be found in the Work and Money section.

Lycos
www.lycos.com or www.lycos.co.uk

The Lycos search engine includes an advanced search option. Lycos also usefully provides it own recommendations. Recommended sites, as chosen by the Lycos site reviewers, are indicated by the Lycos dog logo next to the site review.

MSN Search
www.msn.com or www.msn.co.uk

Microsoft's search site gives you the choice of searching the Web via MSN, Excite or UKPlus.

Netscape

www.netscape.com or *www.netscape.co.uk*

> This search engine enables you to search the Web via Excite, UK Plus and Euroseek as well as via Netscape itself.

Northern Light

www.northernlight.com

> The Northern Light search engine gives you six search options. They include: a simple search, a power search, search news, a business search, an investext search, a special editions search and a geosearch. The special editions search is particularly useful as it contains material exclusive to Northern Light.

UK-specific Web sites

UK Index

www.ukindex.co.uk

> This site is a comprehensive index of UK-based Internet sites. There is a beginners guide and, even more usefully, a job-search engine.

UK Plus

www.ukplus.co.uk

> UK Plus includes search tips and a guide to the Web as well as a work section.

> All of these search engines include a blank search box or form. This is where search words and phrases should be typed. After the terms have been typed and the search button has been hit it will provide a number of links that match your terms. See the next section for more information on keyword searches.

Directories

Excite

www.excite.com or *www.excite.co.uk*

> The Jobs and Careers category includes an advice centre and

salary checker. The subsections are Business, Advice and Guides, By Employer, Industry, For Students, IT Recruitment, Jobs/Career Training, Job and Resume Banks, Labour Relations, Recruitment Firms, Career Services and Women and Business.

Looksmart
www.looksmart.com

The Work and Money section includes the following job subsections: Advice and Guides, For Students, In the Workplace, Job and Resume Banks, Jobs and Career Training, Labour Relations, Recruitment and Regional Careers Resources.

Yahoo!
www.yahoo.com or *www.yahoo.co.uk*

Yahoo!'s employment and work category is in the Business and Economy section. As Yahoo! is a directory it organises Web sites into subject categories (similar to a telephone directory such as the *Yellow Pages*). A good place to start would be the job category section. After clicking through to this section you will be faced with the following options:

◆ *Career Fields* – linking to different career sectors such as Advertising and Marketing, Computers and Science.
◆ *Company Job Listings* – a list of major companies that offer job vacancies at their sites.
◆ *Directories* – providing a list of job-search Web sites.
◆ *Job fairs* – linking to Web sites focusing on job fairs.
◆ *Seasonal and Summer Employment* – linking to information on commercial and summer camps and employment for backpackers.
◆ *Usenet* – provides a list of the discussion groups that centre around employment topics.

Each Yahoo! subsection includes a number in a bracket. The number relates to the total number of Web sites there are in the subsection.

Specialised search engines

To find specialised search engines use:

♦ Invisible Web (*www.invisibleweb.com*);
♦ Search Engine Guide (*www.searchengineguide.com*).

Keyword searches

The most popular method of searching the web involves using keywords to find the information you want. Although, on the face of it, keyword searching seems straightforward it is in fact a fine art. Here are some guidelines to help you conduct effective searches:

♦ *Be specific.* Try to be as specific as possible when entering keywords or phrases into search boxes. The aim with any search is to be as precise as possible so you are not overwhelmed with (the amount of material that the search engine returns with many of the results being completely irrelevant). Search words such as 'employment', 'jobs' and 'careers' are too vague to be used on their own as the search return lists for such words will be very lengthy.

♦ *Use multiple keywords.* Try to think of a number of words that relate to your search topic. It is a good idea to brainstorm before you start in order to be armed with a long list of relevant keywords to type into the different search engines.

♦ *Use suggestions.* Some of the major search engines assist you in this process by providing keyword suggestions. For instance, in their 'Related Searches' section, Alta Vista suggests likely combinations of keywords based on the keyword you have typed.

♦ *Think about word order.* Remember with keyword searching that your first word is normally given priority over the rest.

♦ *Avoid common words.* Try not to use common words such as 'and', 'but', 'if' and 'the' because they really slow search engines down and ensure your search return list is infinitely vast.

♦ *Use lower case.* It is safer to type your searches in lower case although most search engines will search for both lower and upper case, if you use upper case letters, search engines will only search for keywords written in capital letters.

Search results are usually listed (10 to 20 per page) in descending order. If the link looks relevant (there is normally a short sentence that describes the Web site or a list of keywords) then simply click on it and it will take you to the relevant web page.

Use the back button on your Web browser to get back to your search results. Most browsers highlight the links that you have already clicked through which helps when you have a long list of Web pages to look at.

Figure 1 outlines the basic steps involved in a simple keyword search.

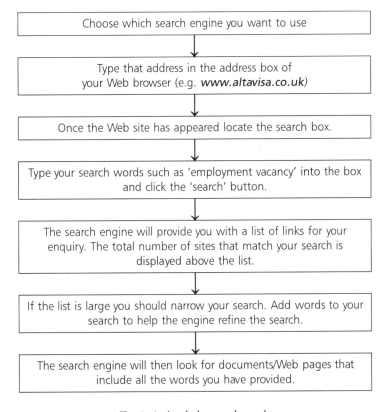

Fig. 1. A simple keyword search.

A keyword search with Google.com

Google is one of the largest search engines in the world and so

provides a good example for a keyword search. In order to look for a recruitment agency which offers marketing vacancies in Manchester the keywords 'marketing', 'vacancy', 'manchester', 'uk', 'recruitment', 'agency' are used to narrow the search.

Here are the query results from Google:

Marketing	12,100,000
Marketing vacancy	78,500
Marketing vacancy manchester	2,050
Marketing vacancy manchester uk	1390
Marketing vacancy manchester uk recruitment	817
Marketing vacancy manchester uk recruitment agency	434

Marketing is the first word that is typed because it is the most important word in the search and word order is vital when searching. This example shows the more keywords that are typed the narrower the search and the results are much more focused.

Secure Searching

Be cautious when searching the Web. Unfortunately, as in the real world, there are some unscrupulous people on the Web. You may think you have found exactly what you are looking for but ask yourself these questions first:

♦ *Is the Web site secure?* If the Web site asks for any kind of personal information or payment from you check it is secure before providing any contact or payment details. More advanced computers often show 'secure' and 'non-secure' warnings when you enter a site but if this facility is not provided here are some of the signs to indicate a Web site is secure:
   – an 's' following the http part of the Web address;
   – a closed padlock sign at the bottom right-hand corner of the browser;
   – a Truste Scheme or Which? Scheme logo (for UK sites only).
If the Web site contains none of these you should be wary about providing any personal information.

♦ *Does the Web site provide real-world contacts?* Check that the Web site includes real world contacts such as an address and telephone number. If anything goes wrong you may need these details.

◆ *Is the Web site official?* If the Web site is not well designed and does not have an official looking domain name it may not be an official site. Also, if you know the company you are looking for make sure all the logos match the offline versions.

◆ *Will your personal details be sold to marketing companies without permission?* Most of the larger organisations state that they will not sell your details to anyone else or at the very least provide a clause which gives you the option to opt out of such arrangements. If there is no such statement or clause avoid providing your details or prepare to receive a mountain of junk mail.

Natural Language Searches

One of the easiest ways to search the Web is by carrying out a natural language search. This involves typing a question or sentence in plain English rather than providing a string of keywords. The most well known English search is available at Ask Jeeves (*www.askjeeves.co.uk* or *www.askjeeves.com*) but AltaVista (*www.altavista.co.uk* or *www.altavista.com*) also offers plain language searching.

Ask Jeeves

Ask Jeeves includes an 'Are you New to Ask Jeeves' section which guides you through eight steps to successful plain English searching. Jeeves supplies much more focused answers if you write sentences rather than single words. After you have clicked the Ask button Jeeves asks you a number of confirmation questions. You should choose the one that most resembles your original question and click Ask. If the question includes a drop-down menu, click on the downward arrow to open the list and choose the item that interests you. Jeeves provides results that people who asked a similar questions thought were useful and also a selection of search engines' top 10 answers to the questions.

Plain English searching with Ask Jeeves

If you typed the question: 'Where can I find a marketing job in Manchester?' Ask Jeeves returns the following:

Please help me clarify your question by selecting from the list below:
♦ Where can I find marketing jobs online?
♦ Which companies offer jobs in marketing for recent graduates?
♦ Where can I find publications that advertise jobs relating to marketing?
♦ Where can I find the popular job search site fish4jobs?

People with similar questions have found these sites useful:
♦ Jobsite. The Award Winning UK Jobs Databases *recommended*
♦ UK IT Jobs

I have found these sites through other search engines:
♦ 9 matches by Mirago
♦ 10 matches by Yahoo
♦ 8 matches by AltaVista

Having clicked the Ask button next to 'Where can I find marketing jobs online?' the site links to the Michael Page International Web pages which offer 25 marketing jobs in the North of England.

Learning to 'Meta-search'

Using more than one search engine improves your chances of finding exactly what you are looking for. However, meta-search engines search the major search engines for you. So instead of hopping from one search site or another to find what you are looking for you can use a meta-search site. Meta-search engines will provide you with larger results (as they are searching more sites) so you should be very specific when you type your query. Here are brief overviews of some of the best meta-search sites:

Mamma.com
www.mamma.com

Mamma.com searches AltaVista, Yahoo!, Excite, Infoseek, Lycos, Web Crawler and HotBot. You can restrict your searches to page titles only.

Metacrawler
www.metacrawler.com

Metacrawler searches 12 of the best engines on the Web (including AltaVista, Infoseek, Web Crawler, Lycos,

Thunderstone, Yahoo! and Excite). The site is very fast and returns a huge amount of data for each query. Metacrawler also offers a 'Power Search' option.

Savvy Search
www.savvysearch.com

Savvy Search is one of the broadest meta-search sites. It searches through Alta Vista, Excite, Direct Hit, Galaxy, Google, HotBot, National Directory, Thunderstone and Web Crawler.

Search.com
www.search.com

CNET's Search.com searches over 700 general and specialist search engines, Web directories and discussion groups.

Other meta-search engines include **Dogpile** (*www.dogpile.com*) and **Profusion** (*www.profusion.com*).

Narrowing Your Search

There are a number of special search commands which can help to narrow searches further than a string of keywords allows. The majority of the major search engines accept the commands outlined here but each search engine is different. Certain search engines are looked at here but further information can be found in the help sections of the major search engines. It is therefore a good idea to read each search engine's instructions before you start.

The plus (+) symbol

The plus (+) symbol tells the search engine that you only want to view pages where both keywords appear. So, if '+ marketing + jobs + vodafone' was typed the search engine would return pages that included all three words.

Placing the plus (+) sign in front of your word search ensures that all your return results will include the first word. If you do not use the plus (+) sign the results may contain some of the keywords but not necessarily all of them. It is a good idea therefore to place the most important word at the front of the list. For example when the words 'design manufacturing employment uk' were typed into Google the return results were in excess of 16 million. When the plus (+) sign was added ('+design + manufacturing + employment + uk') the search results were below 100,000. However this search result would still be too high and further search commands would be required.

The minus (−) symbol

The minus (−) sign (as you may expect) does exactly the opposite of the plus (+) sign. If '+ marketing + jobs − vodafone' was the query the search engine return list would include sites which used the keywords 'marketing' and 'jobs' but not the word 'vodafone'.

The phrase search: quotation marks ("") and dashes (−)

If a list of keywords are placed in quotation marks search engines will only find pages where the words appear in exactly that order. For example "marketing + jobs + vodafone" would only return pages that had the phrase in that exact order.

Some search sites allow phrase searches with dashes (but there must be no spaces in between the dashes). Therefore the 'marketing jobs vodafone' phrase should be typed like this: 'marketing-jobs-vodafone'.

Some search engines such as Alta Vista use 'automatic phrase detection' so you do not need to use the quotation marks or dashes.

Boolean searching

Some search sites (e.g. Alta Vista) recognise so-called Boolean commands such as the words OR and NOT.

The NEAR function finds keywords that are close to each other. The number of words vary between different search engines. For example, 'employment' 'NEAR PriceWaterhouse Coopers' will find matches for Web pages where the word 'employment' is only words away from 'PriceWaterhouse Coopers'.

AND works exactly like the + symbol.

NOT works exactly like the − symbol.

Most search systems allow you to use some kind of Boolean

search. Please note that Boolean commands must always be capitalised.

The 'domain:' command

The domain command offers the ability to narrow searches by concentrating on search engine Web page domain endings. The '+domain:co.uk' will only return searches with .co.uk Web site suffixes. The '–domain.co.uk' search results will include all Web sites except those with a .co.uk address.

The procedure works for all domain endings. So if you are looking for an accounting job in Australia use the search:

"accounting job" + domain:au

Other domain endings include:

.org a non-profit-making organisation
.gov a government department or agency
.net an organisation that deals with the Internet or
  networks (often used in place of .com)
.ac an academic institution
.mil a military organisation

Country specific suffixes include:

.at Austria
.be Belgium
.ca Canada
.cn China
.dk Denmark
.fr France
.hk Hong Kong
.jp Japan
.in India
.hl Holland
.no Norway
.de Germany
.ie Ireland
.nz New Zealand
.za South Africa

For more suffixes check out *www.whatis.com.*

The 'title:' command

If you type 'title:job search' you will only return search results that have job search in their Web page title.

The 'url:' command

The 'url:' command limits the searches to Web site addresses.

The 'text:' command

The 'text:' command limits a search to actual text, as opposed to image titles and links.

The wildcat command (*)

The wildcat command allows you to search for American and English spellings together such as 'colo*r'. Singular and plural spellings can also be searched for at the same time, for example 'dog*'. Also, if you are uncertain about spellings the wildcat command can be used such as 'psyc*ology'.

Combining the symbols

The symbols can be combined to narrow the search further. An example would be:

"Marketing vacancy" – "vodafone London"

This would find all sites that include the words marketing and vacancy except any that were based at Vodafone in London. The return results will be much more manageable if the advanced commands are used together.

Searching by Job Type

Searching by job type and sector can be tailored further to your requirements by using a specialised search engine or directory. As mentioned earlier in this chapter there are a number of specialised subject directories and search engines.

Lists of subject *directories* can be found at:

About.com	*about.com*
Clearing House	*www.clearinghouse.net*

Virtual Library   *www.vlib.org*

Comprehensive lists of subject specific *search engines* can be found at:

Beaucoup   *www.beaucoup.com*
Search Engine Colossus   *www.searchenginecolossus.com*

Directories are very useful when you want to browse the Web but do not know exactly what you are looking for. For example if you were looking for a job in the education sector in the UK you can follow these categories at Yahoo!:

Home > Regional > Countries > United Kingdom > Business and Economy > Employment and Work > Jobs > Career Fields:

This would take you to the following options:

Advertising and Marketing
Computers
Dental
Education
Environment
Financial Services
Government
Health
High Tech
Hospitality
Law
Nursing
Physicians
Science

As you can see the education sector is listed and further links are provided in that section.

Searching by Area

To search jobs by area locate a localised search engine. A list of localised search engines can be found at *www.beaucoup.com/1geoeur1.html* and Spark Search at *www.sparksearch.co.uk*.

Directories are again good resources to search by area. For instance, Looksmart's UK directory enables you to find regional career resources. If you were looking for jobs based in the West Midlands you could go to Looksmart and take the following course of action:

Follow the links:

> Work and Money>Jobs>Regional Career Resources
> ↓
> The site then offers four options:
> England/Northern Ireland/ Wales/Scotland
> ↓
> If you click on the England option the following choices appear:
> London/East/East Midlands/North East/North West/South East/South West/West Midlands/Yorkshire and Humber
> ↓
> Having clicked on West Midlands five site links appear:
> Hereford and Worcester Careers Service
> Shropshire Careers Service
> Shropshire Star
> Staffordshire Careers
> Warwickshire Quality Careers

Searching by Company Name

If you know the company you are looking for you could use a company search engine or white pages. White pages are like telephone directories and may be able to help you locate company e-mail addresses, telephone numbers and Web sites. The most popular include:

BigFoot	*www.bigfoot.com*
Four 11	*www.four11.com*
Whowhere	*www.whowhere.com*
Yell (Yellow Pages)	*www.yell.co.uk*

Company search engines list all companies online. They include:

Companies Online	*www.companiesonline.com*
Hoovers Online	*www.hoovers.com*
World pages	*www.worldpages.com*

If you know the company you are looking for you can often guess their domain name. Most company Web sites follow a formula similar to this:

Prefix→Company name→Suffix
e.g. http://www.sony.com

Prefix

http://www.

Virtually all company Web sites include this at the beginning of their address.

Company name

For example:

Gap
Sony
Orange

Type the name of the company/organisation you are looking for after the prefix.

Suffix

All Web site addresses have a suffix which represent either where the company is based or what type of web site it is. (See above for a list of major suffixes.) Most of the major companies have purchased the .com suffix. For example Orange.com's homepage has links to its sites in Switzerland, the United Kingdom, Australia, Hong Kong, the Dominican Republic, India and Israel.

It is important to note that some organisations have different Web sites for different countries. For example, Sony.co.uk is a completely different Web site to Sony.com but both are owned by the Sony Corporation.

Also watch out for company names that are the same. For example, Gap.com is owned by the clothing company Gap, but Gap.co.uk is an IT solutions business.

Errors

When you are searching the Web you may come across page errors. The most common error you are likely to receive is the 'File not Found' error. This means you will not be able to access that particular Web page. Here are some of the reasons why this may be, as well as some possible solutions:

◆ If the URL you are looking for cannot be located, perhaps the page does not exist anymore or there is a mistake with the URL spelling.

◆ The HTML document you are looking for could have changed. For example, if a link such as *www.tesco.com/ marketingvacancies.html* returns a 'File not Found' page this is probably due to the page having been moved or deleted. The best option is to delete *marketingvacancies.html* in your browser address bar at the top of the screen and press enter/ return. This should lead you to the Tesco Web site and you can search for the vacancy from there.

◆ Occasionally you may not be able to access Web sites because the host server is too busy. Try again later.

◆ Check you are still connected to the Web. If you can access another site then there is a problem with the URL. If not, reconnect and try again.

◆ There may be technical problems with your ISP. In this case contact your ISP's support staff.

Prioritising Information

When you have found the Web sites you are looking for you have to decide what you want to do with all the information. You can:

Read the information online

Although you can read the information online and copy down what you require, this is often time consuming (not to mention costly if you have to pay for your Internet connection time).

Print the page

If you want to print the whole Web page click on the printer

icon of your Web browser if available or choose the 'File'
option and then 'Print'. Certain Web pages cannot be printed
and normally the site will have a link to a printable version.

Copy and paste the page

If the Web page has a lot of graphics or it does not print well
you can cut and paste the text you want to print. To copy and
paste you simply have to highlight the text and choose the 'Edit
Menu' and then press 'Copy'. This pastes your text onto a
clipboard. To view the text you must open up a new word
document in Microsoft Word and choose 'Paste' from the 'Edit
Menu'.

Save the page to your hard drive

To save the Web page to your hard drive choose 'Save As' from
the 'File Menu' and click 'Save'. You can also save Web pages
to your floppy disk drive by following the same process and
choosing A: as your drive option.

Bookmark the page

One of the main ways to avoid 'information overload' is to lay
down markers so you can quickly return to relevant Web pages.
When you've found a good job site, your browser enables you
to store the addresses or URLs of your favourite pages. This will
help you compile your own directory of most visited sites. In
Netscape these are called 'Bookmarks' and in Internet Explorer
'Favourites'.

The way these functions work is simple. When you want to
go back to a particular page, you can go there in one click
instead of trying to remember where it was that you got there
from, or even having to recall a very long Web address. It's
important to remember to bookmark all pages which seem
very useful for your job search, or seem like they might be
useful in future.

Adding a bookmark or favourite couldn't be easier. When
you are at a site you wish to come back to, just click your
mouse on the 'Bookmarks' or 'Favourites' menu at the top of
the screen and move down to select 'Add Bookmark' or 'Add

Favourite'. To get back to a bookmarked page, you need to return to the same menu and select the page you want to revisit by clicking the mouse button.

Of course, if you use the bookmark functions on a regular basis, you may need to arrange your favourite Web pages into separate folders. You can create a folder for each category of bookmark by using the 'New Folder' function, then drag and drop the bookmarks into the appropriate folders. If you have a large number of bookmarks, you can even create subfolders. You can also rename existing bookmarks, delete old ones, or find out the last time each one was visited.

Note: Keep in mind copyright issues when cutting, pasting and printing text from Web pages.

CASE STUDY _____

Rajesh looks for training courses

Rajesh believes he will have to receive additional training to gain a special needs position. He has heard via the Google newsgroups that a good course is available through the Open University; however, he would prefer a course that was based at one of the universities in the North East of England.

He decides to search for relevant institutions via a large search engine. He uses the Google (*www.google.com*) Web site and his first search only contains the one keyword (university). This returns over a million results which is obviously far too many to search through. Rajesh narrows his search by using the keywords '''university tyne+wear special+needs teaching uk'''. This returns six hundred results, and enables Rajesh to locate and apply for suitable courses.

Rajesh is accepted onto a course for special needs training at the University of Newcastle. _____

Checklist

To make your job searching more effective:

♦ *Be specific.* Do not just use one keyword for a search. Use different combinations of keywords.

♦ *Use different search engines.* Do not rely on one search engine because different search engines use different databases. Try the 'meta-search' engines which search different engines at once to save time. Also try localised and specialised search engines to narrow your search.

◆ *Try plain English searches.* If keyword searching produces no relevant results try 'plain English' searching.

◆ *Use search commands.* Search commands add more focus to your searches. The main search commands include : +, −, "", NEAR, AND, NOT, OR, title:, url:, domain:, text:, *.

◆ *Organise your information.* Create your own directory of sites using the Bookmark or Favourites facility on your Web browser.

CHAPTER 7

Using e-mail in Your Job-hunt

E-mail is the single most frequently used application on the Internet. Although the World Wide Web will help you to find the relevant information you require, ultimately your online job-hunting success will depend on e-mail. This is because e-mail enables you to interact with potential employers, and tell them about what you have to offer.

Obviously, the first question you need to ask yourself is 'Should I send my application via e-mail?' Although e-mail has obvious advantages there are many instances when a posted application is preferable. For instance, if a job advertisement states that only posted applications will be accepted, it would be foolish to send a copy of your CV via e-mail. Some employers suffering from 'e-mail overload' understandably try and deter job-seekers from sending e-mail based applications. However, you can send e-mail applications when:

- a position is advertised on the organisation's Web site;
- a job advert provides an application e-mail address;
- you are following up an initial enquiry made via e-mail;
- you have completed an online application form and wish to supplement it with further information.

Understanding e-mail

To make the most of e-mail in your job hunt, it will help to have a thorough understanding of how and when it should be used. Although you may use e-mail on a daily basis, it is still worth being reminded of some basic e-mail facts:

- E-mail allows you to send attached files (such as a word processed CV).
- E-mail can be sent using any Internet-enabled device, although the most popular method remains via computer.
- E-mail is more popular than the Web. According to some

reports nine out of ten Internet users log online primarily to check and send e-mail messages.

♦ E-mail messages do not travel direct. They are usually sent via the 'mail servers' of host computers. This means that no e-mail message is ever completely secure.

It is also important to understand how e-mail is used by organisations (i.e. potential employers) in order to know how to make contact. Although electronic mail was around in some form or another for twenty or so years before its use became widespread, it has now overtaken the telephone as the medium of choice for most organisations (both commercial and not-for-profit). The many reasons for the ever-growing popularity of e-mail include the following:

♦ *Cost.* E-mail is by far the most cost-effective communication tool. The cost of a message is independent of the distance it travels.

♦ *Time.* E-mail messages can be sent and received within a matter of seconds and are therefore expected to be responded to on the same day.

♦ *Convenience.* E-mail boxes are able to receive messages 24 hours a day, 365 days a year.

You do not have to be connected to the Internet to receive messages. Furthermore, it is possible to send as many messages to as many people as you want to, at any time or place you choose. Owing to its obvious convenience, many organisations suffer from 'e-mail overload', with inboxes full of unread messages.

E-mail 'Netiquette'

An understanding of Internet etiquette, or 'netiquette', will enable you to avoid the many pitfalls which can be encountered when sending e-mail messages. Owing to the fact that e-mail is still a relatively new medium, particularly when it comes to job-hunting, many people remain unclear over exactly how it should be used. People either act as though they are writing a traditional letter or they write in note form.

People do not read e-mails in the same way as they read a printed letter or CV. Instead, recipients scan electronic messages quickly looking for relevant information. When an employer reads an e-mail message, they may be aware that they have other unread e-mails in their inboxes to reply to. As e-mails are read in a different way to printed documents, it makes sense to write in a different way too. Here is some advice:

♦ *Be brief.* While you must remain polite at all times when contacting employers, it is also important to make your point in as few words as possible.

  Unlike printed text, people don't put an e-mail down halfway through and then return to finish reading it later. With e-mail, you only have one short chance to make the right impression with potential employers.

  When faced with a lengthy amount of text computer users often *scan* rather than read, looking for key words and phrases to get the gist of the message. With shorter messages, however, they are more likely to read all the text. As a general rule, you should try and keep e-mails to under 20 lines in length. This will prevent people having to scroll down to read the end of the e-mail.

  Also short (two- or three-line) paragraphs are suited more to the electronic format than long chunks of text. However, although the accompanying e-mail should be brief, the time spent preparing your application should not. Technology has created a culture of immediacy but the volume of job applications online makes it even more important to spend as much time as possible selling yourself.

♦ *Avoid block capital letters.* Many job-seekers use block capitals in their covering and speculative e-mails (particularly in subject lines) in an attempt to make their message stand out. Although such messages will indeed stand out, they will not command the sort of attention the sender had hoped for. The fact is that typing in capitals is the Internet equivalent of shouting and is a method used by senders of spam (i.e. junk) e-mail. This tactic is therefore unlikely to win you any favours with potential employers.

♦ *Avoid grammatical and spelling errors.* Needless to say, although e-mail is a relatively informal medium, spelling and grammar mistakes make the wrong impression.

Although most e-mail software programs (such as Microsoft Outlook Express) include a spellcheck function, this cannot be relied on to correct everything. While spellcheckers can spot misspelt words they cannot tell if a word is used in the wrong context. For example, if you typed the word 'cat' when it should have been 'car' the spellcheck would not pick it up. Therefore, however short your e-mails happen to be, you should never forget to proofread them before you send them off.

◆ *Use the 'word wrap' function.* Most e-mail software packages include a word wrap function. This allows you to limit your line width to however many characters as you wish. If you want to ensure that potential employers don't have to scroll across to read each line, you should set the word wrap at around 70 characters. If your software program doesn't include a word wrap facility you can keep your line width short by using the 'Return' key on your computer keyboard. By keeping your messages narrow you will also be ensuring that they are not broken up into jagged lines on the recipient's screen.

◆ *Don't send mass e-mails.* The one way to ensure that your e-mail gets deleted before it is read is to send it to lots of different employers. Employers are always going to be more responsive to candidates who have taken the effort to contact them individually. However, if you do ever need to contact lots of people simultaneously (for instance, to research the job market) use the 'Bcc:' (Blind carbon copy) box rather than the 'To:' or 'Cc:' options. This will keep the addresses of each recipient hidden.

◆ *Be clear.* Although you will inevitably want to impress employers in your e-mail messages, you should try and avoid over-formal or obscure language. Recipients rarely read a message twice and therefore e-mail messages should be made as accessible as possible. According to the Campaign for Plain English (*www.plainenglish.co.uk*) clear language is 'something that the intended audience can read, understand and act upon the first time they see it'.

◆ *Avoid shorthand.* Shorthand is becoming increasingly popular in Internet messages. The two most popular forms of e-mail shorthand are acronyms (such as BTW for 'by the way') and emoticons (symbols intended to represent feelings, such as :-) for a smiley face). Both these forms of shorthand should be avoided when contacting potential employers.

♦ *Introduce yourself.* If you are contacting an employer for the first time, you should introduce yourself and your intention straight away. If the recipient has to wait until the second paragraph to find out who you are, they are likely to hit 'delete' before they get there.

♦ *Don't be too informal.* Research shows that the Internet – including e-mails and chatrooms – invites an informal tone of writing. But no employer will take seriously an e-mail application with inaccuracies.

♦ *Ask questions.* Where appropriate, include questions in your e-mail to encourage a response.

♦ *Don't use nicknames.* Many people set up e-mail addresses based on their nicknames. While addresses such as *partyanimal@hotmail.com, madmax@demon.com* or *sexbomb@yahoo.co.uk* may amuse friends they are clearly not suitable when contacting employers. It is much better, if slightly more boring, to use an e-mail address based on your real name such as *jamesh@hotmail. com* or *sarah.smith@yahoo.com.*

♦ *Check the address.* It may sound obvious, but always make sure that you have checked the recipient's address before you send your e-mail. You should always take time to visit the employer's Web site or contact the enquiry desk to ensure you are approaching the right person for the position you are interested in.

♦ *Avoid HTML.* Do not send your e-mails as HTML files.

Covering e-mails

The covering e-mail is your shop window, as it is the first chance an employer gets to see what you have to offer. As the Jobs.co.uk Web site puts it, 'if you don't grab the employer's attention straight away, it's a lost sale'.

This is your opportunity to supplement your application with the reasons why you are the perfect candidate for the job. You must be careful not to repeat any details you have already given on your CV or application, although you should indicate one or two areas that are relevant to the position you want.

Every CV sent via e-mail needs to have a covering message to introduce it. This e-mail message must be able to do the following:

◆ encourage the recipient to open and read the attached CV (if sent as an attached document);
◆ outline, or at least hint at, the content of the e-CV;
◆ persuade the recipient that you are a suitable candidate for the position or vacancy;
◆ back up the comments you make regarding your suitability for the job.

As the covering e-mail is likely to be the first piece of information to be received, it is equally as important as your CV. Its aim is to make sure your CV is seen by the relevant person and to highlight the key points made.

Supplementing an Application Form

There may also be times when you have filled in an online application form and still want to send a covering e-mail at the same time. This will probably be due to the fact that the form does not enable you to express relevant information about your skills or experience. Furthermore, sending a covering e-mail will make it more likely for your application form to be taken seriously and read with interest. However, you should try and make sure that any supplementary e-mails you send are as short and succinct as possible. After all, if a company uses online application forms in its selection process it means they do not want to deal with lengthy, 'free form' applications.

Edward Beesley from **Go Jobsite** (*www.gojobsite.co.uk*) offers the following advice regarding covering and supplementary e-mails:

Keep it simple, short, punchy but formal. Address the recipient by name 'Mr Jones' if possible. Tailor it to the job you are applying for. Use positive language throughout. Either write the letter directly into the body of your e-mail or attach a word file. Ideally do both.

Useful Phrases

Although it is always a good idea to tailor e-mails to the specific needs of each employer, there are some stock phrases which can be used almost universally in your job-hunt.

Outlined below are just some of the phrases which can be incorporated within e-mail messages to potential employers.

At the beginning of the message:

- *in response to your advertisement*
- *following our telephone conversation*
- *I would like to be considered for*
- *I am writing to enquire whether*
- *Having visited your Web site*

In the middle:

- *I am attracted to working for you because*
- *I believe I am a suitable candidate because*
- *as you can see from my CV*
- *I noticed on your Web site that*
- *particularly interested in*
- *the reason for this is*
- *my main skills are*

At the end:

- *if you require any further information*
- *to reiterate*
- *I look forward to your response*
- *I am available for interview on the following dates*

Figures 2 and 3 provide examples of covering e-mails for two different scenarios.

Sending Speculative E-mails

You should not limit your job-hunt to only those companies which are currently advertising vacancies. If a company you are interested in working for apparently has no positions available it may still be worth sending an e-mail about yourself explaining how your skills and experience could benefit the company. In fact, it is often impossible to tell whether a company has any vacancies or not, as many employers do not

To: *rwilson@companyx.com*
From: *cward@hotmail.com*
Subject: Ref: Personal Assistant Position

Dear Anna

I am writing with reference to your advertisement of 2nd March on The Guardian Web site for the Personal Assistant position. I have attached a copy of my CV for your consideration.

As you will see I have had considerable experience of this type of work during my time at University.

My work experience during vacations has helped to develop a number of skills mentioned in the advertisement, in particular computer literacy and meeting deadlines.

Furthermore, I believe I would bring considerable enthusiasm and commitment to the job.

I look forward to hearing from you.

Regards

Charlotte Ward

T: 0191 555 5555

Fig. 2. An example of a covering e-mail for a permanent position.

To: *asmith@company.co.uk*
From: *dbrown@yahoo.com*
Subject: Work placement

Dear Mr Smith

Studying PR at university gives me the opportunity this second year to undertake a work placement in a suitable company. I was attracted to write to your firm because you use a fresh and unorthodox approach to achieving results.

The placement would help me to gain insight into a PR practitioner's practical work, develop a personal perspective, and obtain items for my Portfolio of Achievements, and you will have a chance to give an enthusiastic student valuable work experience and to get some help for free.

You will meet a positive minded, outgoing individual, who loves challenges and who is eager to learn about the practical work of PR. After several trips abroad, where I have lived, studied and worked with many different people, I have developed my teamworking skills, as well as my communication skills. My CV is attached.

I look forward to hearing from you soon.

Regards

David Brown

Fig. 3. An example of a covering e-mail for a work placement.

advertise vacancies at all. Furthermore, speculative e-mails are often put on file by employers for when suitable vacancies crop up. You may even strike lucky and approach an employer the day before a vacancy is advertised.

Here are some general guidelines for sending the right kind of speculative e-mails:

♦ *Research the company.* When making speculative enquiries, it is more essential than ever to express a thorough understanding of the company or organisation you are contacting.

♦ *Identify a role.* You should identify the role you are interested in almost immediately. You should also clarify what you want to achieve – be it a permanent position, a work placement or whatever.

♦ *Get the right contact.* When sending speculative e-mails you must make sure you have the right name and e-mail address of the relevant contact. You should also try and find out how they prefer to be addressed (Mr, Mrs, Miss, Ms or by their first name).

♦ *Ask a question.* As mentioned elsewhere in this chapter asking questions is one of the best ways to solicit a response from potential employers.

Following Up Via E-mail

If you have already applied for a vacancy or have sent a speculative e-mail enquiry, you may decide to send a follow-up e-mail at a later date. For instance, if an employer replied positively to your initial enquiry and promised to get back to you by a certain date, it makes sense to send a follow-up e-mail when that date is reached. Also, if a company tells you that they will keep your details on file, a follow-up e-mail a month or so later will help you to stay in the mind of the employer.

Here are some general guidelines to consider when sending follow-up messages:

♦ *Place the message in context.* Don't assume employers will remember who you are. Always place follow-up e-mails in context by reminding employers of your original e-mail and maybe even quoting from it.

◆ *Be brief.* You want to make sure any follow-up e-mails are as short as possible. There are two reasons for this. Firstly it will ensure the e-mail gets read. Secondly, a long e-mail will give the impression that you are pestering the recipient.
◆ *Offer more information.* While you should make sure your follow-up e-mail is brief, you should also offer further information if required. After all, the employer may no longer have your original application.

Case studies

Trudy's covering e-mail

Dear Annie Pearson

I am writing with regards to your advert for an Internet Marketing Assistant in The Belfast Telegraph (21/3/01).

I am a 24-year-old BA Business Studies graduate who has relevant experience in this field having just completed work experience at 'Internet Marketing Company X'.

I believe working with the largest and most successful Internet Marketing company in Belfast would be an exciting and challenging prospect and is exactly what I am looking for.

Please find my current CV attached (the file was created using Word for Windows 98 Mac Version).

I look forward to hearing from you.

Regards

Trudy Dawn
T: 012 345 678 9870
E: *trudydawn@hotmail.com*

Philip submits his details to a recruitment firm

Philip decides to send his CV and a covering letter to the relevant recruitment executive at Hays. Philip uses his old home computer to type his CV and covering letter documents. Instead of writing a message in the e-mail, Philip sends his covering letter as an attachment and the e-mail is left completely blank.

When the executive receives Philip's CV and covering letter he cannot open the file because Philip's computer software is not compatible with his.

Philip did not provide him with information on the software he used to create the file, and also failed to include a contact telephone number for the executive to let Philip know he cannot access his application. Instead the recruitment executive sends an e-mail to Philip to tell him his problem. He asks Philip to send his CV pasted into an e-mail instead. _____

Checklist

E-mail will be used frequently in your job-hunt. Here are the main best practice guidelines:

- ◆ *Follow the rules of e-mail netiquette.* The rules include keeping to the point, not shouting and avoiding HTML.
- ◆ *Do send follow up e-mails.*
- ◆ *Use the word wrap function.*
- ◆ *Do not use acronyms or emoticons.*

CHAPTER 8

Your e-CV

T he growing use of the Internet as a medium to advertise job vacancies has been met by a rise in the number of Internet-based applications. A few years ago only IT professionals would have considered sending their CV electronically, but nowadays employers and job-seekers from every sector welcome the idea. Indeed, in a recent survey (conducted by NetSource) 81 per cent of employers say they now accept e-CVs. Some company Web sites now ask for all applications to be sent via e-mail. If you find an ideal job vacancy online it usually makes sense to send your CV over the Internet.

CV Basics

There are some rules which apply equally to CVs in the real world and on the Internet. All CVs should *include*:

◆ *Your skills and experience.* Relevant experience and skills form the backbone of your CV. Always remember to match them as closely as possible to those indicated in the job description.
◆ *Your achievements.* Achievements need to be highlighted clearly as employers rarely have time to search in depth.
◆ *Your qualifications.* Employers will need to know your educational profile so make sure you provide them with information on your most relevant qualifications.

All CVs should *avoid*:
◆ *Pretentious language.* Resist using unnatural or over-formal words and phrases. Academic and technical jargon should also be kept to a minimum.
◆ *Lies.* Although it may be tempting to fabricate non-truths to get your dream job, it will do you no favours in the long

term. In fact, there can be hardly anything more embarrassing than being caught out in an interview situation.

◆ *Irrelevant personal information.* Keep unnecessary information to a minimum to let your achievements stand out. Marital status, religion, number of children and gender can, in most cases, be left out.

All CVs should be short, succinct and straightforward. They also need to be clear and easy to read.

Above all this however, you need to make sure your CV is relevant, both to the job and to the company.

Essential Information

Although a CV should be as unique as the person who sends it, the *type* of information which should be included applies to all CVs. Namely:

1. Your full name
2. Your contact details
3. Your date of birth (you should not mention your age separately)
4. Your personal profile
5. A summary of your key skills
6. Your employment history
7. Your (secondary and further) education
8. Any other training
9. Interests

When to Use an e-CV

Web-advertised vacancies usually specify whether they require a postal or an electronic method of application. If they do not specify, use your own discretion. The fact that the post is advertised on the Web will probably mean they are willing to accept Internet-based applications.

Some employers give you the option of submitting a CV or completing their application form. A CV provides you with more freedom, but an application form will provide you with more prompts regarding what the employer is looking for.

The Benefits of e-CVs

If an employer is advertising on the Web it means they want someone who uses that medium. They are therefore likely to welcome e-CVs as proof that you are computer literate and in tune with the Internet age.

Other benefits of e-CV's over their 'real world' counterparts include the following:

♦ *Links.* You can add another dimension to e-CVs by including hypertext links to relevant Web sites. These could be links to the sites of previous companies you have worked for or even of universities or colleges you have attended. To add links into your CV simply place a full Web site address within diagonal brackets such as <*http://www.mylastjob.com*> and save it as 'Rich Text'. This involves clicking on the 'format' option and then choosing 'Rich Text' in your e-mail application. Links to your referees' e-mail addresses may also be added (with their permission).

♦ *Speed.* The Internet enables you to send CVs to an employer's mail box instantly.

♦ *Presentation.* You can be safe in the knowledge that employers will receive the CV in exactly the same condition as when you sent it.

♦ *Cost.* E-CVs save on postage and stationery costs.

♦ *Response.* Due to the fact that e-mail is quick and cost-effective, and that it encourages feedback, it also means employers are more likely to respond. You are also likely to hear sooner rather than later. This will help keep nail biting to a minimum.

According to Edward Beesley, the senior marketing consultant for recruitment site Go Jobsite (*www.gojobsite.co.uk*), the benefits of an e-CV also include the fact that it can be

easily distributed around the world, with no postage cost and once you have the template you can then easily tailor each CV you send out. You can post it on a site such as Go Jobsite and let the employers look for you. The process of job application is much faster as you can send off your CV and have a response within an hour.

Making the Right First Impression

Making the right initial impression has always been an important factor for successful CVs. Employers rarely devote more than a minute to decide whether a CV is worthy of their consideration. With e-CVs, the first impression is even more important. After all the trash can is never more than one mouse click away. E-mail is a fast and immediate medium which requires you to make a good impact within a matter of seconds.

Here are some ways to make sure you make the right first impression.

♦ *Spellcheck.* Make sure you have conducted a spell and grammar check before sending off your e-CV. However, don't rely solely on the capabilities of your word processing program. If you have typed in 'key kills' instead of 'key skills', the spellcheck facility will not pick the error up because your mistaken words are spelt correctly.

♦ *Start with a concise summary of your skills.* This will help to give an employer an overall picture of what you have to offer in a nutshell.

♦ *Have a strong subject line.* The subject line will be the first thing a potential employer will see – it is at this point that they will make a decision as to whether they want to read further. See below for more advice on the subject line.

♦ *Keep it as short as possible.* Although 'curriculum vitae' is the Latin phrase for 'the course of your life' this is exactly what it shouldn't be. Employers don't want *War and Peace* – they want a short and succinct impression of each candidate.

♦ *Combat 'CV fatigue'.* Combat 'CV fatigue' by keeping superfluous information to a bare minimum.

♦ *Write a CV that stands out.* Recognise that you will be miles ahead of the pack if you reproduce different CVs for different jobs. Don't fall into the common trap of regarding your CV as your first shot at autobiography. Its purpose is not to reflect your infinite variety but to beat the other 150 applicants trying to get onto the employer's shortlist.

♦ *Use nouns and action words.* According to Hewlett Packard 'A growing number of recruiters such as ourselves now use software packages to automatically scan and sift online applications according to key words and buzz phrases'.

Making a Maximum Impact CV

Here are some more ways to ensure your CV makes the maximum impact:

◆ *Keep it short.* Explain what you have achieved using short sentences and bullet points – you can always expand on these at the interview stage.
◆ *Practice truth economy.* While it's not advisable to lie in your CV you don't have to include information that will diminish your chance of an interview – as long as it doesn't affect your ability to do the job. Always put things in the best light possible.
◆ *Avoid out-of-date information.* Putting things that happened more than ten years ago down on your CV will make you look as if you have passed your sell-by date, unless they have a direct bearing on your present capabilities.
◆ *Don't include references.* There is no need to put the names and addresses of references on your CV.
◆ *Question your CV.* Go through your CV and assess the information by constantly asking yourself: 'Will this encourage people to interview me?' If the answer is no, you should seriously consider leaving it out.
◆ *Follow the BLUF rule.* The BLUF rule states that you must always put the Bottom Line Up Front, in other words put the most important details at the start of your CV.

Getting the Subject Line right

The strength of your subject line determines whether your e-CV will be read. Here are some basic points to think about when writing a subject line:

◆ *Be brief.* A subject line should ideally be no longer than eight words.
◆ *Avoid overemphasis.* CAPITAL LETTERS AND EXCLAMATION MARKS LOOK LIKE YOU ARE TRYING TOO HARD!!!

◆ *Keep it simple.* If you are responding to an advertised vacancy, keep the subject line direct and simple, such as 'Application for Office Manager position'. If on the other hand you are sending a 'Keep my CV on file' speculative application, you may need to try a bit harder.

◆ *Be correct.* Poor spelling anywhere in an e-mail, and especially the subject line, sends the wrong signals.

Tailoring Your CV

Your CV should always be tailored to suit the specific requirements of each individual job application. When tailoring your CV you should consider the following:

◆ What is one thing you want the employer to remember as soon as he or she sees it for the first time.

◆ Which areas of your skills and experience are most relevant to the application and should therefore be highlighted.

Different formats

The chronological CV

Traditionally there has only been one accepted CV format, the *chronological CV.* This format puts the emphasis on career growth and educational development, presenting information in a reverse chronological order.

To construct a chronological CV begin with your most recent achievements. If you finished full-time education within the last 3–4 years place this information above your career details. If not place career information first.

The functional CV

Increasingly employers are welcoming CVs which focus on skills and abilities instead of just providing a linear history of your career and education. As Steve Davies of online recruitment agency Stepstone.co.uk explains:

The functional CV is rapidly growing in popularity as it can make it much easier for employers to judge a person's credentials at a glance.

For more information on the pros and cons of both formats visit: *http://www.cvsearch.net.*

Making Your e-CV Compatible

e-CVs can either be sent as attachments or pasted into e-mails. With e-CVs your mail-reading software may be different to the recipient's, but there are measures you can take to ensure that your e-CV appears acceptable on all browsers.

Here are some basic guidelines to help you produce a completely compatible e-CV.

◆ *Save it as plain text.* If you are putting together a CV using a word processing program, save it as plain text, then cut and paste it into your e-mail program.
◆ *Make the first screen stand out.* As the sender's name and e-mail address always appear at the top of a message, don't fill the first screen with your contact details. Instead, put them at the foot of the e-mail. Start with either an outline of your career situation or your employment objective.
◆ *Send the CV to your own address first.* This will help you see what it will look like on your target employer's computer screen.
◆ *Consider small screen sizes.* E-mail screens only allow 65–70 characters (including spaces) to a line. Use the word count facility on your word processing program to check the number of characters.
◆ *Give each screen a coherent look.* For instance, avoid screen breaks coming in the middle of a sentence.
◆ *Use a standard font.* Some fonts are unavailable to certain e-mail programs so stick to a standard font such as Times Roman or Arial.
◆ *Use a widely used word processing program such as Microsoft Word.*

Figure 4 provides an illustration of a plain text e-CV.

Top tip: Although you cannot use formatting tools you can highlight text by using characters such as $* = \approx \Delta +$. To italicise text place it between the » and « symbols.

Subject: CLERICAL ASSISTANT APPLICATION
Date: Wed, 15 March 2001 09:21
From: Sally Peacock speacock@hotmail.com
To: jsmith@ocecontracts.co.uk

» PERSONAL PROFILE
A well organised and competent clerical assistant with experience of accounts, order office and general office work. Hardworking and trustworthy, good at handling a variety of tasks efficiently, with the ability to remain good-humoured and unflappable under pressure.

» KEY SKILLS
– Keyboard skills – 60 wpm
– Operating fax machine and photocopiers (Canon and Rank Xerox)
– Preparing and writing routine correspondence
– Dealing with incoming phone calls
– Maintaining records

»KEY EXPERIENCE
–   1998-2000 Rosencrantz and Guildenstein
        – CLERK TYPIST
        – Typing from manuscript
        – Maintaining files
        – Organising appointments
–   1996-1998
        – ORDER CLERK
        – Processing orders
        – Raising order codes
        – Preparing and writing outgoing mail
        – Organising and carrying out routine administration

»EDUCATION
– 1992-1996 Thomas Magnus School
        – 9 GCSEs A-C including English Language

»PERSONAL DETAILS
– Date of birth: 3rd July 1977
– Interests: Riding and pony trekking, reading and cinema.

Fig. 4. An example of a plain text e-CV.

Online Application Forms

A lot of larger firms with a strong Web presence provide you with a ready-prepared online application form.

While application forms can help you to get a picture of what an employer is looking for, they are not without their drawbacks. They are generally intended to gather and to obtain standard information and therefore you may find it difficult to get your 'unique selling points' across. They certainly don't offer you much flexibility in terms of how you present information. What they will do, however, is help you find out whether the firm is the right choice for you (and vice versa) or whether you should apply elsewhere.

Many firms use online application forms as the 'first hurdle' in their recruitment process. They know that less committed candidates seeing a ten-screen application form will be unlikely to make the effort. By not bothering to fill in the form people effectively eliminate themselves from the running, even though they may have the relevant skills and experience necessary. Therefore just by taking the time and effort to complete the form you will be giving yourself a head start.

Specific things to remember about filling in online application forms include:

◆ *Read through the application from thoroughly before you start.* This will help you to make sure you are right for the job and will prevent you from repeating yourself.
◆ *Print off a copy.* Working on a printed-out copy before transferring the details back to the original will make it easier for you to think carefully about the information you provide. Instead of printing, you could copy and paste it into a word processing package.
◆ *Fill in every box.* Incomplete forms are unlikely to get you on the interview shortlist.
◆ *Adhere to any hints, tips and advice the site offers.*
◆ *Submit the form in advance of the deadline.* Most application forms will have a submission date. Try and submit the form at least a few days before the final date.
◆ *Make it relevant.* As with your e-CV, all the information you provide should be as relevant as possible to the job you are applying for.

Getting Help Online

A whole online industry has grown up around advising people on how to compose CVs and covering letters. In fact, many Web sites will actually create your CV for you (albeit at a price) if you type in your details.

The best sources of free help are online careers advice services such as *http://www.jobhuntingonline.com* and *http://www.jobtrack.co.uk*. Although these services will not write your CV for you, they will help you build your own by giving you detailed information, including worksheets and examples.

If you choose to pay to have your CV written, make sure the Web site is qualified for the task. The Internet makes it possible for just about anyone to set up a Web site offering a CV-writing service. One of the best CV services can be found at *http://www.monsterboard.com* which works with you to build a successful and targeted CV and covering letter.

In addition, publicly posted CVs on the Web at sites such as *http://www.cvsearch.net* give you the opportunity to look at how other people have approached the task and to learn from them.

Other useful sites to check out are given below:

Alec's CV Tips
www.alec.co.uk

Packed with free advice on putting together your CV, it also offers a professional CV writing service.

CV Concepts
www.jobfinder.com

Set up by IBM's head of recruitment this site provides CV advice from an employer's perspective.

Professional CVs
www.edinburghconcepts.com/cv_homepage.htm

Provides free CV and form-filling tips.

Checklist

◆ You should send an e-CV if:
- the job is advertised on the Web;
- the vacancy information expresses a preference for online applications;
- the site does not provide an online application form.

◆ When sending an e-CV you should make sure all information is:
- relevant to the job;
- accurate;
- up to date.

◆ To make sure your CV gets read:
- start with a summary of your skills;
- use a strong subject line;
- keep it as concise as possible;
- send the CV in the main body of the e-mail;
- send it to your own address first.

CHAPTER 9

Job-hunting Offline

Although this book has argued that the Internet is a vital resource for job-seekers, it is important to remember that it is only one of several recruitment methods. This chapter looks at the various ways in which you should back up your online efforts with some 'real-world' activity. While some of the methods in this chapter may be seen as optional in your bid to secure the right job, others (such as interviews) are not.

Remember the Real World

Despite the fact that the majority of companies offer information online some do not provide everything you will require on their Web sites.

Although most companies recognise the importance of the Internet for recruitment purposes, very few neglect offline recruitment methods. Newspapers and offline trade publications are still the preferred option for companies wishing to advertise vacancies (although many print titles incorporate their job listing on the Web as well).

Furthermore, while some companies enable job-seekers to apply on their Web site, many more do not. Similarly, while applications sent via e-mail are often accepted, CVs sent via the postal service are often what employers expect to receive. Also, although online interviews are expected to be popular in the future, for the moment at least employers prefer the face-to-face method.

Therefore while the Internet is arguably the most effective way of researching organisations and finding job opportunities, it should not replace offline job-hunting activity.

Researching Offline

Offline newspapers and trade magazines will often provide

vacancy details for relevant positions. Newspapers can be a particularly good way of finding out about local vacancies.

Although most jobs that are listed in newspapers are also included on their respective Web sites, not all local papers will provide this service. If this is the case, check out when the job section appears in your local paper and check it every week for suitable vacancies.

Trade magazines are also a good source of job information if you are searching for work within a particular industry. Here are a few examples of trade titles and the industries they represent:

Accounting Age	Accountancy
Building Design	Architecture and Construction
Computer Weekly	Information Technology
Media Week	Media and Marketing
Press Gazette	Journalism
PR Week	Public Relations

As there are literally thousands of trade titles on the market you may need help locating them. However, most local libraries will stock a media directory such as Brad or Hollis in their reference areas. Getting your hands on trade titles can be difficult as they are not usually stocked in local libraries (although if you have easy access to a business library you will probably find what you are looking for there). Unfortunately, some publications are only available by subscribing on an annual basis.

The best national newspapers for job information are *The Guardian, The Financial Times, The Independent, The Times, The Scotsman* and *The Daily Telegraph*. Many of these newspapers provide job listings relating to particular industries on different days.

There are also free newspapers which are devoted solely to job listings. For instance, *The Career Post* which is billed as 'The Specialist Recruitment Newspaper' publishes thousands of vacancy details every week for industry sectors such as nursing, administration, retail, engineering, IT, insurance, construction, marketing, accounting and sales. *The Career Post* is available in most UK regions and can be picked up at job centres, universities, libraries, colleges, training organisations and even supermarkets.

These newspapers can clearly offer job-seekers relevant vacancy information. Although two or three years ago people were making predictions that every one would eventually only ever find and apply for jobs via the Internet, this no longer seems to be the case. In fact, the amount spent on recruitment advertising in the UK national, regional and trade press is on the rise (the annual spending figure is now in excess of one billion pounds). The reality is that newspapers and the Internet can and should be used in unison together if job-hunters are to maximise their chances of securing a dream job.

Visiting Career Fairs

Careers fairs remain a popular way for employers to make contact with potential employees. These fairs are usually aimed at school and college leavers as well as graduates. Although one or two Web sites, such as **Gradunet** (*www.gradunet.co.uk*), have attempted to replicate the career fair experience on the Internet, there are many benefits of the traditional format.

Perhaps the most obvious advantage of the real-world careers fair is the fact that it provides job-seekers with a chance to talk to employers face to face. This form of contact serves as effective interview preparation and also offers the opportunity to make a good impression at an early stage in the recruitment process.

Careers fairs also help you to see how the recruitment process really works. While it may sometimes seem that the ball is in the employer's court, the careers fair puts the picture straight. At these events employers are often falling over themselves in order to speak to job-seekers. While you may be intimidated by your competition, you will get a true picture of the choice of work opportunities on offer.

While the main aim of a careers fair (from a job-hunter's perspective) is to find useful information on different companies' employment schemes, they also provide invaluable networking possibilities. However, in order to get the most out of the event you should carry out a bit of research before you get there. If you can find out which companies are going to be attending the fair, you will be able to assess who you want to speak to in advance. You should also take a few copies of your

CV along to give to any employers who are interested.

Once you realise which companies are attending the event, you will be able to come up with some questions to ask employers. This will not only help you to find out useful information about the company, but will also convey a positive sense of enthusiasm and interest.

There are two main types of careers fair: general and specialised. General fairs are aimed at anyone seeking employment and will feature a wide variety of organisations and companies. Specialised fairs, on the other hand, will be aimed at a specific group of people (e.g. graduates) and may concentrate on one industry sector (e.g. travel and tourism).

To find out about careers fairs you should keep a look out in local newspapers and trade publications. You should also check the notice boards in your college or university (if applicable). The **Give Me a Job** Web site (*www.givemeajob.co.uk*), **Gradunet** (*www.gradunet.co.uk*) and **Reed** (*www.reed.co.uk*) also provide information on forthcoming career fairs and similar events.

Employment and Careers Services

To maximise your chances of securing the right job you will need to visit employment and careers services offline as well as online. These services perform two main functions as they are a source of both vacancy information and useful career advice.

By far the largest employment organisation in the UK is the Civil Service's Employment Services. Employment Services oversee the local employment offices and job centres which are situated throughout the UK. If you are out of work, Employment Services provide you with a client advisor who can help you find suitable vacancies as well as possible advice on benefits and training.

For those still in further education (or just out of it), university and college career offices can be a useful source of information. These offices often feature useful books, career overviews, information on interviews and psychometric tests, further education details (MAs, doctorates, etc.) and vacancy details. You will also be able to make an appointment with a career counsellor who will be able to talk you through the job options you face.

Careers offices are not just the preserve of academic institutions as they can also be found in the centre of most large towns and cities. Furthermore, local libraries normally include a careers section and often have staff who can help with general careers enquiries. Needless to say, all of these services are free of charge.

Sending Postal Applications

Many companies still prefer candidates to send applications by post rather than via e-mail. In fact, some organisations only accept posted CVs and application forms. The most important thing to remember, as always, is to play by the employer's rules.

Find out exactly how candidates are expected to apply (by post or online?, CV or application form?) and stick to it. If you cannot find out from their Web site, contact the company direct and ask.

Printed CVs

While most of the rules for e-CVs mentioned earlier in this book apply equally for the printed CV, you should also adhere to the following advice:

♦ *Use quality paper.* Posted CVs should be word processed on quality white or light cream paper.
♦ *Use a clear typeface.* The clearest font to use for e-CVs is Helvetica which is easily read on a computer screen. With offline CVs, however, Sans Serif or Times Roman should be used.
♦ *Stick to two sides.* CVs should never be longer than two sides of A4 paper.
♦ *Use the insert-table tool.* The 'insert table' tool on your word processor will make your CV look more professional than if you rely on the tab key. (This applies to e-CVs as well if they are sent as an attached word file.)
♦ *Correct mistakes on your computer.* Although you will need to print out a copy of your CV to proofread it, you should make corrections using your computer. Amendments made by hand using a pen or Tip-Ex clearly make the wrong

impression.

Covering Letters

If you are sending a CV via the post, you will need to put together an accompanying letter. As with covering e-mails these letters provide you with the opportunity to tell the employer why you are the right candidate for the job. You should start by introducing yourself and specifying which vacancy you are applying for (as well as how you heard of it). The rest of the letter is then taken up with outlining and supplementing the information in your CV. As with their e-mail equivalent, covering letters should not be too long.

However, while the basics remain the same, there are some obvious points of difference between cover e-mails and letters, such as:

◆ *The date.* While the time and date at which you send an e-mail appears automatically when the recipient opens the message, the same is not true for letters. When writing a covering letter you therefore need to include the date at which it was sent. This goes at the top right-hand corner of the letter below your address, and should be written in full without abbreviations, for example '12 December 2001'.

◆ *The address.* While it is not necessary to include your address on an e-mail cover message (providing it is included in your CV), in a printed covering letter you will need to include it in the top right-hand corner above the day's date. You should also include the employer's full address in the top left-hand corner slightly below your own address.

◆ *The greeting.* While many Internet-friendly companies are starting to accept the more informal greetings encountered in e-mails, the 'Dear Mr Smith' (or whoever) format should obviously be adhered to in printed letters.

◆ *The sign off.* Again, while a degree of informality is accepted in e-mail sign-offs (such as 'Regards'), covering letters should adhere to the formal rules of business letter writing. If you know the recruiter's name you should close the letter with 'Yours sincerely', and if you don't know the name use

'Yours faithfully' instead.

◆ *Use one side.* Covering letters should never be longer than one side of paper.

As with printed CVs it is always important to use quality paper and a clear typeface, as well as to correct any mistakes using your word processor.

Application Forms

Application forms are used by some companies in order to make sure that the information a candidate provides remains directly relevant to the positions applied for. More and more companies are offering their candidates the opportunity of filling in an application form online. **Marks and Spencer** (*www.marks-and-spencer.com*), **Unilever** (*www.ucmds.com*), **Scottish Power** (*www.know-us.co.uk*), **Royal and Sun Alliance** (*www.royal-and-sunalliance.com*) and **Dyson** (*www.dyson.com*) are just a handful of the companies which now have online application forms at their Web sites.

Having said that, the majority of organisations which use application forms only provide a printed option. However, the principles involved in both offline and online form filling remain the same. These are outlined below:

◆ *Practise your response.* Not all the questions on the form will be immediately obvious. Some will require a significant amount of thought in order to make the right impression. If you are filling in a printed form you should use a photocopy to fill out your responses in rough first. This will ensure that you will not have to make corrections on the form itself.

◆ *Follow the instructions carefully.* Make sure you follow the instructions carefully before answering each question. For instance, the employer might instruct you to write all the answers in black ink or block capitals.

◆ *Be honest.* Although it may be tempting to exaggerate in order to sound more impressive, you need to remember than you may have to expand on your responses in an interview situation.

◆ *Stick to the deadline.* Most application forms will include a final date for submission. If you go over that deadline your application will be automatically discarded.

◆ *Don't leave gaps.* Blank spaces on application forms give the employer the impression that you have nothing to say about yourself and should therefore be avoided. If you are allowed to submit more information on a blank sheet of paper, it can be a good idea to do so providing what you have to say remains relevant to the question.

◆ *Be original.* Application forms are intended to help you express your originality. When you are competing with a lot of candidates (and you inevitably will be) make sure that your responses will stick in the recruiter's mind.

◆ *Proofread the form.* Recruiters look for easy ways to screen out the weakest applicants. Spelling and grammatical inaccuracies will provide them with a legitimate excuse to reject your application.

Assessment Centres

Assessment centres are one of the most daunting aspects of the offline job-hunt. They are often used by companies before the interview stage of recruitment as a way of filtering out unsuitable candidates. Although some companies incorporate assessment centres into the interview stage itself, sometimes candidates will be asked to attend assessment centres after an initial interview.

Increasingly assessment centres are being used by companies wanting to see how candidates can work in a team. The reason why assessment centres have become so popular is because of the growing belief that interviews are not a one hundred per cent reliable way of choosing the right person for the job. Typically, a day at one of these centres will involve the following exercises:

◆ *Group tasks.* Candidates are usually divided into separate groups to perform a certain activity. This helps employers assess each candidate's teamwork skills.

◆ *Psychometric tests.* These are often in the form of a written exam with multiple choice questions.

◆ *Personality questionnaires.* These tests are intended to assess personalities and the candidate's 'Emotional IQ'.

♦ *Mock situations.* Often candidates will be faced with a mock situation which is similar to what they could encounter during a typical working day.

Assessment centres are used by companies such as Marks and Spencer, Tesco and Powergen and many other large UK companies. In an article which appeared in *The Guardian* newspaper Stewart Jackson of Powergen explains how assessment centres work:

> An assessment centre would take on a similar style each time we use it ... We often include ability tests. Psychometric testing tends to be verbal or numerical reasoning and frequently includes an Occupational Personality Questionnaire (OPQ). We then use either group exercises or an individual presentation, as well as a competency-based interview.

Most of the experts seem to agree on the best piece of advice for candidates: don't panic. Of course, this is easier said than done but the thing to remember is that assessment centres are not there to highlight your weaknesses. The main aim is to see what you are good at. Although the first time you go to an assessment centre can be rather scary, many candidates actually enjoy their second visit.

The Interview

When you are told that you are required to attend an interview, you are likely to feel a mixture of excitement and apprehension. Your application details have shown the employer that you have the skills and experience required – now you have to indicate that you can back up claims made on paper in real life.

However, from the outset it is important to remember that an interview is a two-way process. Just as the employer is looking to see if you are right for their company, so too are you assessing if the company is right for you.

Be prepared

The motto for interview success is simple: be prepared. You will need to be able to provide good answers for most (if not all) of the interviewer's enquiries, as well as have a few questions of your own. As mentioned elsewhere in this book, the Internet can help you find out more information on a company and the industry within which it operates. This knowledge can prove very useful in an interview situation.

Obviously it is impossible to predict exactly what the interviewer will ask you, although it is reasonably safe to assume the questions will follow three themes, namely:

◆ *Your suitability for the role.* The primary concern for the employer is to find out whether you are capable of doing the job.

◆ *Your experience.* The employer is likely to draw on areas of your CV or application form which refer to your education and experience. The task you face in the interview is to try and bring these points to life by explaining their relevance to the job. The employer ultimately wants to get a picture of who you are.

◆ *Your compatibility.* Just because you have the skills and experience required doesn't mean the employer will think you are the right person for the job. They will be looking to see whether you will be able to fit in with the company's culture. This is also something you too should be concerned with: is the company right for you?

Possible Questions

Here are some examples of questions which relate to one or all of these three areas:

◆ Why do you want to leave your current job?
◆ What are you hoping to get out of this role?
◆ Tell us about your analytical skills.
◆ What are your main weaknesses?
◆ Where do you see yourself in five years' time?
◆ Why do you want to work for us?
◆ What attracted you to this position?
◆ How would you describe your relationship with colleagues?

While all of the above questions are relatively predictable, you must also watch out for the 'killer' question. In an interview you should always expect the unexpected. Employers occasionally like to catch you off guard in order for you to reveal your true colours.

Office Angels, the secretarial recruitment firm, published an interview report in October 2000 that claimed that over 75 per cent of the employers questioned admitted to asking tricky questions. These included:

♦ What do you see as the major trends in our industry?
♦ If you were a merry-go-round, what music would you be playing? (This is an actual question used regularly by one employer to gauge the interviewee's creativity.)
♦ Would you ever lie in the interests of your job?
♦ Can you name five members of the Cabinet?
♦ Give me three things to remember you by.
♦ Tell me a joke.

Although you should always try to answer the interviewer's questions, if you do not have a suitable response or if you did not understand you should say so. If nothing else, the employer will appreciate your honesty.

More Interview Tips

Here are some further interview tips you should take on board:

♦ *Use real examples.* All too often candidates resort to vague and abstract answers which bear no relation to their real experience. By drawing on specific things which have happened rather than on hypothetical possibilities, you will be more likely to convince an employer of your capabilities.
♦ *Dress for the job.* When you are deciding what to wear think of the job (and company) you are applying for. While it may be acceptable to dress in casual clothes if you are going for a job at a trendy Web design company, it is unlikely to be suitable for an interview with an accountancy firm or legal practice. However, you must always try and feel comfortable in what you are wearing.
♦ *Relax.* Although an interview is an unusual situation, you

should try to relax and act yourself. After all, if you pretend to be someone you are not you are not going to do yourself or the company any favours in the long term.

◆ *Be inquisitive.* As mentioned earlier, an interview is a two-way process. By asking questions you can find out useful information at the same time as expressing your interest in the company.

Case studies

Trudy prepares for her interview

Trudy is asked to attend an interview at one of the most prestigious marketing companies in Belfast. She opts to research the company and industry in more depth, and so she decides to search the marketing industry press to see if the company has been mentioned recently.

Using the Internet, she manages to locate an article in *Marketing* magazine about the company just winning two huge Internet client accounts. She also finds an article in *Marketing Week*, written by the director of the company, which talks about the need for change in the Internet marketing industry. Trudy agrees with the director's viewpoint and is pleased to be going for an interview with such a forward-thinking company.

In the interview, Trudy is asked if she knows anything about the company and she explains that having read both *Marketing* and *Marketing Week* (this indicates to the interviewer that she has a keen interest in the industry) she knows of the two new account wins. She also makes clear that she is aware of the company's philosophy which she is completely in agreement with (this shows she is interested in the company and not just interested in the money that the job would bring).

Trudy is offered the job.

Philip practises psychometric tests online

Philip receives a letter from one of his 'top companies' that he would like to work with and is invited to an interview. The letter explains that he will be asked to complete a psychometric test at the interview.

Philip has never undertaken a psychometric test before and is uncertain as to what he should expect. He locates psychometric tests on the Internet at sites such as Assessment (*www.assessment.com*) and ASE (*www.ase-solutions.co.uk*). Philip practises using the psychometric tests and also finds out from the sites what the answers actually mean in terms of accountancy employability.

When Phlip is asked to take a test at his interview he is surprised that it is virtually the same psychometric test that he has come across on the Internet. Philip not only knows what he should answer but also what each answer means to the employer. Owing to his online practice it is not surprising he passes the psychometric test. _____

Checklist

As well as using the Internet, you will need to do the following in order to maximise your chances of securing your dream job:

- ◆ Look at job vacancy information in the national, regional and trade press.
- ◆ Visit career fairs.
- ◆ Use 'real-world' employment and careers services.
- ◆ Send CVs, covering letters and application forms via the post when an online alternative is unavailable.
- ◆ Prepare thoroughly for your interview using both online and offline methods.

Appendix

Getting Online

As the Internet becomes ever more popular, the means of accessing it become ever more varied. The Internet is now available via TV sets, mobile phones and PDAs (Personal Diary Assistants) as well as desktop computers. However, for job-hunting purposes the desktop PC (or Mac) remains the most convenient option.

What You Will Need

Outlined below are the five things you should have in order to benefit fully from the job-hunting opportunities offered by the Internet – a computer, a modem, a Web browser, an Internet service provider and an e-mail account.

A Computer

Although the Internet is now available via mobile phones and the TV as well as the desktop computer, a computer is still essential if you plan to do your job-hunting online. The Mac versus PC debate is no longer really that important. A few years ago if you bought a Mac, it would mean that a lot of useful software would be unattainable by you. Nowadays, most major software packages can be used on Macs as well as PCs and so this is less of an issue.

A more significant point you need to consider concerns the computer's power. The more RAM a computer has, the better, as it will mean your computer will be able to work faster, be able to use more software packages and crash less often.

A Modem

To connect the computer to the Internet you will need a modem. Increasingly, computers are becoming equipped with internal modems, although external modems are still available. Most modems basically do the same job, the only way of telling them apart is in terms of transfer speed. This refers to how quickly data can be transferred into audio files and other formats. This speed is measured in kbps (kilobytes of information per second). For most purposes your modem should run at a minimum of 56 kbps.

A Web Browser

Web browsers are by far the most vital and popular piece of net software, as they enable users to access Web documents and download useful information. Without a Web browser your computer will not be able to display Web pages or any other HTML files (HTML stands for Hyper Text Markup Language – the computer coding used to create Web sites and other graphical documents).

As well as Web access many Web browsers also include significant extras such as e-mail and newsreader programs. Microsoft Internet Explorer and Netscape Navigator are the most popular browsers available, and one of them is likely to come free with your computer or through your Internet Service Provider.

Internet Explorer also includes e-mail, a newsgroup reader and a Web authoring package. The two major Web browsers also include features which can prove particularly useful for online job-hunting, such as bookmarks enabling you to store the addresses of useful Web sites you want to return to.

An Internet Service Provider

To get the most out of the Internet you will need to choose an Internet Service Provider (ISP). As their name suggests, ISPs provide a range of Internet services designed to make Internet access and use a lot easier. However, as well as providing fast Internet access, many ISPs offer services such as e-mail accounts and Web space. Most importantly an ISP acts as an intermediary, providing the software needed for a modem to dial and connect to the Internet. There are literally thousands of ISPs out there offering all manner of services, and so choosing the right one can be a nightmare. However, it is important that you think long and hard before making a decision.

Before deciding on an ISP, you will need to know how reliable they are, how quick their download times are and how effective their e-mail services are.

When choosing an ISP you need to consider the following points:

◆ *Access.* You will need to make sure the ISP you use has good access via the phone network (no engaged signals or slow transmissions).

◆ *Support.* Most ISPs offer a support service. Make sure the person you deal with on the phone understands and is interested in your requirements. Check the helpline by phoning up with some questions. If the line is difficult to get through to or the representative is impatient or impossible to understand take your custom elsewhere. Also, make sure that you check the call rate charges. Many ISPs charge over 50p a minute for using their customer hotline.

◆ *Newsgroups.* It is important to make sure that the ISP you choose carries all the newsgroups in Usenet, as these groups (as mentioned earlier in this book) can provide valuable networking and research opportunities.

◆ *E-mail.* If you want your ISP to provide your e-mail account you will need to consider their e-mail options.

◆ *Browsers.* Although most ISPs only support Microsoft Internet Explorer, some (such as Compuserve and Netscape Online) also provide Netscape options.

◆ *Cost.* The monthly subscription charge varies greatly between different ISPs.

Remember that if you end up having to change ISPs at some later stage, significant costs may be involved in making the transfer.

ISP Listings

BT Internet
www.btInternet.com

BT's ISP, as you might expect, is also rather popular. Its choice of software is based on Microsoft's Internet Explorer.

Clara Net
www.claranet.net

Clara Net is one of the leading consumer ISPs and offers the easiest installation procedure imaginable. All it involves is clicking on a link marked 'I want to join Clara Net' on the Clara Net Site. Unlike most of the major ISPs Clara Net also offers a choice of Netscape as well as Microsoft Web software.

Demon Internet
www.demon.net

Demon Internet was awarded the title of 'Best ISP on the planet' by *Internet* magazine in 2000 (it had been runner-up the year before). It was judged the ISP most suited to virtually every level of Internet experience and expertise. Demon is particularly famed for its efficient technical support. It offers a 30-day trial, a beginner's booklet, and the option to uninstall existing accounts.

Primex
www.primex.co.uk

Relaunched in 2000, Primex now offers fast and flexible installation as well as a vast range of browsers and Web tools available.

Here are some more ISPs worth checking out:

AOL	*www.aol.co.uk*
Compuserve	*www.compuserve.co.uk*
Connect Free	*www.connectfree.net*
Easy Net	*www.easydial.co.uk*
Freedom 2 Surf	*www.freedomtosurf.com*

Line One	*www.lineone.net*
MSN	*www.msn.co.uk*
Netcom	*www.netcom.net.uk*
Netscape Online	*www.netscapeonline.co.uk*
Supanet	*www.supanet.co.uk*
Virgin	*www.virgin.net*
Which? Online	*www.which.net*
World Online	*www.worldonline.co.uk*
X-Stream	*www.x-stream.co.uk*

More information on ISPs can be found at the NetBasics site (*www.netbasics.com*), an independent Internet advisory service.

An E-Mail Account

E-mail will play a very important part in your job-hunt as you may use it to communicate with potential employees as well as other job-seekers. In fact, in all likelihood you will spend more time on e-mail than on any other area of the Internet. You will therefore need an account which is reliable (sending and receiving messages on time) and user friendly.

If you use an ISP e-mail account, the provider will give you an installation CD-ROM and addresses you need to configure your e-mail software. The main problem with ISP-based e-mail addresses is that they are linked to the service provider you have chosen, so if you change to a different ISP, you are likely to lose your addresses.

The other option is to use a Web-based e-mail service such as Microsoft's Hotmail (*www.hotmail.com*), Lycos Mail (*www.lycos.com*) or Yahoo! Mail (*www.yahoo.com*). This type of service has two obvious advantages. It is free and, as it is not linked to any subscription from a provider, your e-mail address remains the same even when you change ISP. The fact that it is not linked to an ISP also means that messages can be sent and received from any computer with access to the Internet.

There are, however, certain drawbacks with Web based e-mail accounts. You are generally more likely to be sent 'spam' (i.e. junk) e-mail messages if you subscribe to a free Web-based service. Furthermore, Web-based services also tend to be less secure than other forms of e-mail and you must always remember to log out of your e-mail Web page. The other disadvantage, which will not really affect your job-hunting efforts, is that there is often limited space on your account when you use a Web-based service.

Accessing the Internet without your own computer

If you do not own a computer or have a computer that cannot access the Internet, take advantage of your local library or Internet café. The majority of local libraries have computers with free Internet access and also support staff who can help you set up an e-mail account and guide you through the Internet. Most universities, colleges and schools provide computers with free Internet access for their members.

Internet cafés can be found in most major towns and cities. Internet cafés usually charge by the minute or hour, although prices are generally very reasonable. For example, Virgin has launched it's own Internet café called Virgin Space and (at the time of writing) they were offering an Internet deal of £1 for a whole day surfing. The advantages of using a library or Internet café is that help is always at hand and they are very reasonably priced.

Directory of Useful Web Sites

Business Directories

Ask Alix
www.askalix.com

> Ask Alix is an online directory of over one million UK companies enabling you to search by keyword, name or town.

Big Yellow
www.bigyellow.com

> Big Yellow is a compilation of most of the *Yellow Pages* directories around the world.

The Biz
www.thebiz.com

> Biz stands for 'Business Information Zone' and The Biz Web site conducts searches based on industry, location and the alphabet.

British Companies
www.britishcompanies.co.uk

> The British Companies site includes links to governing bodies, institutions and associations.

City Pages
www.citypages.co.uk

> City Pages is a UK-based directory of commercial links which categorises information by postal code areas.

Click4itlocal
www.click4itlocal.co.uk

> This directory is aimed to help people locate local businesses.

County Web
www.countyweb.co.uk

> A searchable database of UK businesses which, as you might expect, are divided into separate counties.

Dun and Bradsheet
www.dunandbrad.co.uk

> This site claims to have the most up-to-date definitive database of company information in the world. It includes a global directory of over 500 million businesses in 230 countries. The company information includes business name, address, nature of business, number of employees and annual turnover. Even more usefully (for job-hunting purposes at least) it can provide you with a list of all the companies within a particular location, in a specific industry or of a certain size. Furthermore, each list includes the relevant contact names. However, only certain aspects of this service are free.

Infoseek
www.infoseek.co.uk

> Although Infoseek is a general search engine it also includes a very useful business directory. Thousands of company Web sites are classified under areas such as advertising, banking, employment, manufacturing, marketing, e-commerce, media and telecoms.

The Internet Pages
www.the-internet-pages.co.uk

> The UK's A to Z of businesses and services (as well as sales, repairs, hire and entertainment).

Kelly's
www.kellys.co.uk

> Kelly's is a long-established directory of over 14,000 UK companies providing contact details. Registration (which is free) is required before you can access the site.

Scoot
www.scoot.co.uk

Scoot's vast database incorporates 2 million records, over 3,000 business categories and 27,000 locations. The site enables you to search for companies either by name, location or business sector.

UK Business Net
www.ukbusinessnet.com

UK Business Net is a business-to-business information resource which includes a financial index, a business data file, events diary and industry reports.

UK Pages
www.ukpages.co.uk

UK Pages is an extensive database of UK businesses with direct links to company Web sites.

UK Plus
www.ukplus.co.uk

UK Plus is a directory and search engine owned by the *Daily Mail* which indexes a wide variety of UK Web sites.

Yahoo! Business and Economy
www.yahoo.co.uk

Yahoo!'s Business and Economy listing is probably the most popular UK business directory. The section has links to business libraries, business opportunities, classifieds, courses, electronic commerce, finance, marketing, Web directories and perhaps most significantly employment.

Yell
www.yell.com

The *Yellow Pages* site is an easy-to-use, comprehensive guide to thousands of UK Web sites. Each one has been reviewed by a team of researchers.

Interview Advice

Adecco Alfred Marks
www.adecco.co.uk

> The Adecco Alfred Marks Web site includes a comprehensive interview section divided into the following areas: preparation, at the interview, after the interview, interview challenge and case studies.

Alec's Job Interview Advice and Techniques
www.alec.co.uk

> This unique online resource provides an extensive amount of job interview advice, including interview techniques, questions the interviewer may ask you, questions you may want to ask the interviewer, general interview guidance, panel interview and group interview tests. The 'job interview questions you may be asked' section is particularly useful, including classics such as 'Why do you want this job?', 'What do you know about this company?' and 'Do you know how to motivate other people?'

Graduate Recruitment
www.graduate-recruitment.co.uk

> Interview advice from this graduate recruitment agency.

Haybrook's Interview Advice
www.haybrook.co.uk

> Although aimed at IT professionals, Haybrook's interview advice is of value to all job-seekers. Among the nuggets offered is the following piece of advice: 'Plan to arrive 5–10 minutes before your allotted interview time. Arrive too early and you could put your interviewer under pressure, arrive late and you would put yourself under pressure.'

Matchmaker
www.matchmaker.co.uk

> Matchmaker provides job-seekers with 10 golden rules for handling interviews, including examples of questions you may want to ask the interviewer.

Monster
www.monster.co.uk

> Monster's Career Centre provides extensive advice in its 'Interview Tips' section. The guidelines on body language are particularly useful and informative (here is one example: 'If there's more than one interviewer, look at who's talking').

CV Help

Alec's CV Writing Tips
www.alec.co.uk

> Comprehensive CV guidance from one of the best job advice sites. The site features a number of useful CV examples.

University of London
www.careers.lon.ac.uk

> The University of London's Web site includes a career section with advice on how to target your CV to specific employers.

Monster
www.monster.co.uk

> Monster's CV and cover letter resources include 'Dos and Don'ts', 'FAQs' and a useful section entitled 'Your value in the job market'.

Reed
www.reed.co.uk

> Reed includes CV writing advice on its Web site.

Skillsgroup
www.skillsgroup.ie

> Useful advice from the Irish recruitment agency Skillsgroup on how to write the perfect CV.

Self-assessment sites

2h
www.2h.com

Assessment Matters
www.assessment-matters.org.uk

Career Influences Survey
www.topjobs.co.uk

Career Mapper
www.ti.com

CareerWeb – Employment Search Readiness Inventory
www.cweb.com

CareerStorm
www.careerstorm.com

Emotional Intelligence
www.utne.com

Jobs
www.jobs.co.uk

> Online self-assessment section including 'Career Advantage'
> which provides specific information to assist in career choices.

Leaders Direct
www.leadersdirect.com

> Online questionnaire on leadership, self-esteem and
> assertiveness.

Milkround
www.milkround.com

Mind Tools
www.mindtools.com

National Association for Managers of Student Services in colleges.
www.namss.org.uk

> A collection of links to online test sites.

NFER-NELSON
www.nfer-nelson.co.uk

The Platinum Rule
www.platinumrule.com

Reed
www.reed.co.uk
>   Reed's psychometric assessments will help you choose your career. The interactive quiz entitled id60 has been designed to find out your personality at work and the 'Job Satisfaction Index' analyses your relationship with your job.

Self Discovery Workshop
www.iqtest.com
>   Take a free IQ test at this site. This site is the Internet's most popular and entertaining IQ test.

Selfgrowth
www.selfgrowth.com

SHL Direct
www.shldirect.com

Total jobs
www.totaljobs.com
>   Total job's 'Career Health Check' finds out what jobs are a perfect match for you.

True Globehopper
www.labourmobility.com

Workthing
www.workthing.com
>   Assess your CV at this site.

Search Engines

AltaVista
www.altavista.co.uk

Excite
www.excite.co.uk

Google
www.google.com

Infospace
www.infospace.com/uk

Looksmart
www.looksmart.co.uk

Lycos
www.lycos.co.uk

Northern Light
www.northernlight.com

Ukmax
www.ukmax.com

UKplus
www.ukplus.com

Webcity
www.webcity.co.uk

Worldonline
www.worldonline.co.uk

Yahoo!
www.yahoo.co.uk

Trade Magazines and Journals

Accountancy Age
www.accountancyage.co.uk

Accountancy Magazine
www.accountancymag.co.uk

Accounting, Auditing and Accountability Journal
www.mcb.co.uk

Air Transport Intelligence
www.rati.com

Architectural Review
www.arplus.com

Arts Business
www.arts-business.co.uk

British Medical Journal
www.bmj.com

Caterer.com
www.caterer.com

CFO Europe
www.cfoeurope.com

Communications International
www.totaltele.com

Computer Weekly
www.computerweekly.co.uk

Construction News
www.cnplus.co.uk

Construction Plus
www.constructionplus.co.uk

Current Archaeology
www.archaeology.co.uk

Daily Telegraph
www.telegraph.co.uk

DotElectronics
www.electronicstimes.com

DotPharmacy
www.dotpharmacy.co.uk

Electronics Weekly
www.electronicsweekly.co.uk

Financial Times
www.ft.com

Future Publishing Online
www.futurenet.com

Health Club Management
www.health-club.co.uk

Health Service Journal
www.hsj.co.uk

Housing Today
www.housingtoday.org.uk

Information for Industry
www.ifi.co.uk

Inside Housing
www.insidehousing.co.uk

Leisure Week
www.leisureweek.co.uk

Marketing Online
www.marketing.haynet.com

Marketing Week
www.mad.co.uk

Media Week
www.mediaweek.co.uk

Nature
www.nature.com

New Civil Engineer
www.nceplus.co.uk

New Media Age
www.nma.co.uk

New Scientist
www.newscientist.com

Next Wave
nextwave-sciencemag.org/uk/

Personnel Today
www.personneltoday.net

PR Week
www.prweekuk.com

Public Finance
www.cipfa.org.uk

Surveyors Plus
www.surveyorsplus.co.uk

The Business
www.thebusiness.vnunet.com

The Lancet
www.thelancet.com

The Law Gazette
www.lawgazette.co.uk

The Stage
www.thestage.co.uk

Times Educational Supplement
www.tes.co.uk

Regional Press

Channel Islands

The Guernsey Press and Star
www.guernsey-press.com and www.thisisguernsey.com

Jersey Evening Post
www.jerseyeveningpost.com and www.thisisjersey.com

East Anglia

Cambridgeshire
Cambridge Evening News
www.cambridge-news.co.uk

Peterborough Evening Telegraph
www.thisispeteboroughet.co.uk

Norfolk and Suffolk
Eastern Daily Press and East Anglian Daily Times
www.ecn.co.uk

East Midlands

Derbyshire
Derbyshire Times
www.derbyshiretimes.co.uk

Leicestershire
Leicester Mercury
www.thisisleicester.co.uk

Lincolnshire
Lincolnshire Echo
www.thisislincolnshire.co.uk

Northamptonshire
Northamptonshire Chronicle and Echo
www.northamptonshireecho.co.uk

Nottinghamshire
Nottingham Evening Post
www.thisisnottingham.co.uk

North

Cleveland

Evening Gazette
www.eveninggazette.co.uk

The Hartlepool Mail
www.hartlepoolmail.co.uk

Tyne and Wear

Evening Chronicle
www.evening-chronicle.co.uk

The Journal
www.the-journal.co.uk

Sunderland Echo
www.sunderland.com/echo and www.sunderland-echo.co.uk

North West

Lancashire

The Blackpool Citizen
www.thisisblackpool.co.uk

Lancashire Evening Post and Wigan Evening Post
www.lep.co.uk

Manchester

Bolton Evening News
www.thisislancashire.co.uk

Manchester Evening News
www.manchesteronline.co.uk

Merseyside

Daily Post and Liverpool Echo
www.liverpool.com

Northern Ireland

Belfast Telegraph
www.belfasttelegraph.co.uk

Belfast Irish News
www.irishnews.com

Republic of Ireland

The Dublin Irish Times
www.irish-times.com and *www.ireland.com*

Scotland

Central

Dundee Courier and Advertiser
www.dcthomson.co.uk

Daily Record
www.record-mail.co.uk

The Herald
www.theherald.co.uk

Grampian

Press and Journal
www.thisisnorthscotland.co.uk

Aberdeen Independent
www.aberdeen-indy.co.uk

Tayside

Dundee Evening Telegraph
www.dcthomson.co.uk

South West

Avon

The Bath Chronicle
www.thisisbath.com

Bristol Evening Post
www.thisisbristol.com

Devon

Evening Herald (Plymouth)
www.thisisplymouth.co.uk

Express and Echo
www.thisisexeter.co.uk

Herald Express (Torquay)
www.thisissouthdevon.co.uk

Western Morning News
www.westernmorningnews.co.uk

Wales

News Wales
www.midwalesonline.co.uk

Wales Daily Post
www.liverpool.com

West Midlands

Hereford and Worcester

Evening News (Worcester)
www.thisisworcestershire.co.uk

Shropshire

Shropshire Star
www.shropshirestar.com

Staffordshire

The Advertiser
www.thisisstaffordshire.co.uk

Express and Star
www.westmidlands.com

The Sentinel
www.sentinel.co.uk

Warwickshire

Warick
www.warickonline.co.uk

West Midlands

Coventry Evening Telegraph
www.iccoventry.co.uk

South East

All

Evening Standard
www.thisislondon.co.uk

Berkshire

Reading Evening Post
www.reading-epost.co.uk

Essex

Essex Chronicle
www.thisisessex.co.uk

Herts and Essex Newspapers: Essex Observer, Mercury, Harlow Star
www.herts-essex-news.co.uk

Hampshire

The News
www.thenews.co.uk

Southern Daily Echo
www.dailyecho.co.uk and *www.thisishampshire.net*

Oxfordshire

Oxford Mail
www.thisisoxfordshire.co.uk

East Sussex

Brighton Evening Argus
www.thisisbrighton.co.uk

Yorks/Humbershire

Humbershire

Grimsby Evening Telegraph
www.grimsby-online.co.uk and *www.thisisgrimsby.co.uk*

Hull Daily Mail
www.hulldailymail.co.uk and *www.thisishull.co.uk*

Scunthorpe Evening Telegraph
www.thisisscunthorpe.co.uk

North

York Evening Post
www.thisisyork.co.uk

Scarborough Evening News
www.scarborougheveningnews.co.uk

South

The Doncaster Star
www.sheffweb.co.uk

Yorkshire West

Huddersfield Daily Examiner
www.ichuddersfield.co.uk

Telegraph and Argus (Bradford)
www.telegraph-and-argus.co.uk

Yorkshire Evening Post
www.yorkshire-evening-post.co.uk

Yorkshire Post
www.ypn.co.uk

Recruitment Sites

Agency Central
www.agencycentral.co.uk

> Agency Central allows candidates to search for an IT agency by name, county and skill-set. CVs can also be submitted online and distributed to all subscribed agencies.

All Freelance
www.allfreelance.com

> Freelance jobs and resources for telecommuting professionals.

Apply4it
www.apply4it.co.uk

> Offers services for Berkshire, Thames Valley and the South East provided by local independent recruitment agencies.

Appointments For Teachers
www.aft.co.uk

> UK teaching vacancies.

Appointments Plus
www.appointments-plus.com

> The Telegraph's recruitment site.

BigBlueDog
www.bigbluedog.com

> London vacancies.

Brook Street
www.brookstreet.co.uk

> Secretarial, office and light industrial recruitment.

CareerMosaic
www.careermosaic-uk.co.uk

> Job database, mainly IT positions.

Charity People
www.charitypeople.com

> The Charity People Recruitment Consultancy.

City Jobs
www.cityjobs.com

> The site specialises in Financial, Media, IT and Legal jobs.

Compurecruit
www.uk.compurecruit.com

> IT jobs.

DotJobs

www.dotjobs.co.uk

> General recruitment.

e-job

www.e-job.net

> Advertising, marketing, PR and sales jobs.

Easy Jobs

www.easy-jobs.co.uk

> Providing employers and job seekers with tools to communicate directly.

Engineers Online

www.engineers-online.co.uk

> Engineers Online is the UK's leading engineering portal with a highly active job site.

First Division Jobs

www.firstdivisionjobs.com

> First Division Jobs is an interactive recruitment Web site advertising over 1,000 jobs. They cover secretarial, professional, IT and marketing positions. Candidate profiles are advertised for employers and agencies to search.

Fish4Jobs

www.fish4jobs.com

> Vacancies covering all industries with job news, recruiter information and career advice.

Freelance H.Q.

www.freelancehq.com

> The only independent IT agency review site in the UK.

GAAPweb

www.gaapweb.com

> Specialises in finance and accountancy vacancies.

Gis-a-Job
Gisajob.com

> Gis-a-Job has thousands of UK job vacancies and covers all industry sectors. Also provides an e-mail job alert service for job-seekers.

GoJobsite UK
www.gojobsite.co.uk

> One of the largest vacancy databases.

Golden Square
www.goldensquare.com

> Recruitment consultants for IT, secretarial, design, new media and legal.

GraduateLink
www.graduatelink.com

> Offers graduate jobs, employer profiles, online CVs and training for graduates, and recruitment agency services for businesses.

Gradunet
www.gradunet.co.uk

> Information for graduates including details of graduate vacancies.

IT-pages
www.it-pages.co.uk

> IT jobs and careers searchable with a database from recruitment agencies. Also information, resources, links and services for the IT industry.

JobCity
www.jobcity.com

> Job database of IT positions.

JobHunter
www.jobhunter.co.uk

> Job vacancies from local and regional newspapers throughout the UK.

JobPilot
www.jobpilot.co.uk

> The Web site includes jobs throughout the UK and world-wide. It has more than 50,000 job offers. Job-seekers can receive job offers by e-mail.

Jobs AC UK
www.jobs.ac.uk

> The site specialises in academic appointments.

Jobs.co.uk
www.jobs.co.uk

> Jobs.co.uk is the UK's premier jobs portal. Job-seekers can save time by using the unique meta-search engine to search 40 of the top job sites simultaneously. In addition, there is a database of over 500 UK vacancy sites in all sectors and locations, links to hundreds of employers, CV and applications advice and many more job-seeker resources.

JobSearch
www.jobsearch.co.uk

> You can select jobs by location as well as type.

JobServe
www.jobserve.com

> Job database with thousands of permanent and contract IT positions.

JobsNetwork
www.jobsnetwork.co.uk

> Large job database.

Jobs Unlimited
www.jobsunlimited.co.uk

> UK database of jobs from *The Guardian* newspaper.

Jobworld
www.jobworld.co.uk

> Job database with vacancies for people looking for work in IT, banking and finance, sales, medical and engineering. You can also search a multi-industry job database or register to receive the latest jobs by email.

Just Engineers
www.justengineers.net

> Engineering vacancies recruitment site, offering job search, career advice, newsletters, links and e-mail alerts.

Monster
www.monster.co.uk

> The Godzilla of recruitment sites.

NetJobs
www.netjobs.co.uk

> Job database with thousands of jobs from major UK recruitment agencies.

Network Design
www.sonnet.co.uk/network

> Vacancy details for graphic design, interior design, design management and architecture.

Overseas Jobs
www.overseasjobs.com

> This site contains all the resources you could possibly need for finding a job overseas. Their database for international job-hunters contains at least 1,500 overseas job vacancies of all kinds.

Pathfinder
www.pathfinder-one.com

> Career transition & jobhunting resources for the UK.

People Bank

www.peoplebank.co.uk

> Job database with over 5,000 jobs covering all fields.

PhD Jobs

www.phdjobs.com

> Combines careers advice with vacancy lists specifically relevant for postgraduates.

PlanetRecruit

www.planetrecruit.co.uk

> UK and International recruitment database.

Premier Employment

www.premier-employment.co.uk

> Premier Employment is an agency for temporary and permanent jobs throughout the South West of England.

Price Jamieson

www.pricejam.com

> Media, marketing and communications vacancies in the UK and world-wide.

Purple Moves

www.purplemoves.com

> Aimed at travellers and professionals travelling and working in the UK, Australia, New Zealand, South Africa and Ireland.

Quantum Jobs

www.quantumJobs.com

> Offers job listings from recruitment agencies and headhunters, e-mail notification of vacancies, and résumé/CV posting forums.

Recruitment Scotland

www.recruitmentscotland.com

> Lists a range of jobs in Scotland.

Recruit Online
www.recruit-online.co.uk

> Recruit Online has a comprehensive directory of UK recruitment agencies which are searchable by industry sector.

Reed.co.uk
www.reed.co.uk

> UK's leading employment agency with thousands of vacancies online, including computing, accountancy, office and secretarial, graduates, insurance, banking, healthcare and technical.

Silicon
www.silicon.com

> This site specialises in IT vacancies.

Siteworkjobs
www.siteworks.co.uk

> Database for skilled and experienced site workers, employers and agencies.

StepStone
www.stepstone.com

> Offers a wide range of job vacancies in all professions throughout the UK and Europe.

Taps
www.taps.co.uk

> The Taps database includes jobs in: IT, engineering, graduates, accountancy, banking and finance, general business, human resources, management, marketing, media and advertising, publishing, project management, retail and sales.

Top Jobs on the Net
www.topjobs.co.uk

> Job database with job adverts from leading UK firms including: accountancy and financial management, banking and finance, consultants, customer service, engineering, executive and management, graduates, health, human resources, information

technology, legal, logistics, marketing, media, production and operations, public sector, retail, sales & business development, scientific.

UK IT Contractors.com
Ukitcontractors.com

UK IT Contractors.com provides a direct recruitment service for UK-based computer contractors.

WayGoose Selection Ltd
www.waygoose.com

Provides recruitment services to the printing and graphic arts industries.

Womenback2work
www.womenback2work.co.uk

Womenback2work.co.uk is the complete online resource for women returning to work, providing course information, help on job searching, childcare advice and even guidelines on starting your own business.

WorkWeb
www.workweb.co.uk

Jobs in the following fields: admin/secretarial, banking, catering, construction, education, electrical/electronic, engineering, executive/management, accountancy and finance, health, human resources, insurance, information technology, legal, manual, media, marketing, other professional, production, personal/security, retail, sales, scientific, travel and transport.

Industry Recruitment Agency Sites

Accountancy/financial

ABPM
www.abpm.co.uk

ABPM is a recruitment agency specialising in the recruitment of senior finance staff, with offices in Nottingham, Leeds,

Manchester and Birmingham. The company's financial recruitment division provides a permanent and a temporary recruitment service across all business sectors on a local, national and international basis.

Accountants on Call
www.aocnet.com

This international company specialises in temporary appointments for jobs in banking and accounting. The company has a network of over 100 offices throughout the UK, Canada and the United States. Each candidate is personally and extensively interviewed, usually by two staffing experts.

Badenoch and Clark
www.badenochandclark.com

An accountancy, banking, investment management, law and IT recruitment agency with branches covering all of the UK. Their recruitment service is free of charge to candidates, whose details are stored on an extensive database.

Beament, Leslie, Thomas
www.blt.co.uk

BLT provides recruitment consultancy services for clients involved in direct tax, indirect tax and company secretarial service.

DLA Recruitment Consultants
www.dla.co.uk

DLA Recruitment Consultants specialises in financial and IT recruitment and is based in London.

Executive Match
www.e-m.co.uk

Executive Match is an accountancy recruitment firm with a vast database of financial jobs. The site's candidate zone incorporates a useful search function which enables visitors to search the extensive vacancy database.

Finance Professionals
www.financeprofessionals.com

> Finance Professionals has specialist teams placing candidates at many different levels within a company. According to the FP Web site: 'Our candidates range from Part Qualified Accountants through to Corporate Finance Directors and we have consultants that are specifically trained to work at those different levels.'

FSS Financial
www.fss.co.uk

> The FSS site enables visitors to search for available jobs, up-to-date news, client information and job-search advice.

Greenwell Gleeson
www.greenwell-gleeson.co.uk

> This Midlands-based recruitment firm employs more qualified accountants as consultants than any other agency in the area.

Hays Accountancy Personnel
www.hays-ap.com

> As one of the largest accountancy recruitment organisations, Hays has the most comprehensive database of permanent temporary and contract accountancy professionals and support staff in the country. As the site puts it: 'with 125 offices, we've got the nation covered'.

HH Financial Recruitment
www.hhrecruit.com

> A specialist finance and accountancy consultancy with offices in London, Birmingham and Sussex.

Hitchenor-Maher
www.hitchenor-maher.co.uk

> Specialising in accountancy and financial services recruitment.

Howlett Thorpe
www.howlett-thorpe.co.uk

> Focuses on accountancy recruitment in commerce, industry and public practice.

Indigo Selection
www.indigoselection.co.uk

In February 2001, City recruitment consultants Indigo Selection and temporary accountancy specialists Hewitson Walker merged to provide one single financial recruitment service covering both permanent and temporary positions. Each division of Indigo Selection is divided into teams covering specialist areas of the financial markets. The consultants themselves also work in their own areas based on a specific client portfolio or on defined vertical sectors. The accountancy and finance division recruits at all levels from accounts clerks to financial directors across various sectors including investment banks, other financial service organisations and blue-chip commercial companies.

Michael Page
www.michaelpage.net

A long-established agency Web site enabling users to search by region and job type.

Morgan-McKinley
www.morgan-mckinley.co.uk

Specialising in accountancy, banking and IT, Morgan-McKinley is one of the fastest growing recruitment consultancies in the UK. According to a Morgan-McKinley spokesperson: 'Our unrivalled track record in recruiting high-calibre candidates for the top banks, large financial institutions and FTSE 100 companies has given us an enviable reputation.' Their Web site includes a Career Services section which provides accountancy job searches with information on building your CV and successful interviewing through to securing the right job.

Morgan West
www.morgan-west.co.uk

Based in Bristol, Swindon, Cheltenham and Cardiff, Morgan West handles permanent, temporary and contract accounting recruitment. The Web site has general accounting divisions as well as an Internal/International Audit division and Executive search and selection division for senior finance executives in the UK.

Nicholas Andrews

www.nicholas-andrews.co.uk

> One of the UK's leading specialist financial recruitment consultancies. According to the Web site the company's success in meeting the needs of an ever expanding and increasingly demanding market-place is evidenced by 400% growth (1998–2001).

Tover Graham

www.tover-graham.co.uk

> An agency specialising in permanent and contract accountancy recruitment.

Wade Macdonald

www.wademacdonald.com

> Accountancy recruitment agency with offices in the South of England.

Construction

Calco

www.calco.co.uk

> A technical recruitment agency specialising in building and property, civil engineering and quantity surveying.

Construction Plus

www.constructionplus.co.uk

> Popular construction industry portal with news and jobs in all sectors of the industry.

Eden Brown

www.edenbrown.co.uk

> A recruitment agency which specialises in most aspects of the building and construction sector. The Eden Brown Web site incorporates a comprehensive job search database.

Good Building Jobs
www.goodbuildingjobs.com

> Good Building Jobs is an employment portal and job notice board for the construction industry, not an employment agency. This is a free service.

Hays Montrose
www.haysmontrose.co.uk

> Hays Montrose claim to be the UK's largest and most successful construction and property recruitment specialists. The range of construction roles the company recruits for include project manager, site manager, civil inspector, clerk of works, health and safety officer, document controller, quantity surveyor, commercial director, buyer and material scheduler, planner, land buyer, marketing and sales staff. The company's clients include Wimpey Homes, Bovis Homes, Barratt Homes, Balfour Beatty, Crest Homes, MJ Gleeson and the Wates Building Group.

Hill McGlynn
www.hillmcglynn.com

> Hill McGlynn has a long history of recruiting construction professionals. The company has a branch network with bases in London, Birmingham, Manchester, Bristol, Leeds, Southampton and Welwyn Garden City. Each branch has teams assigned to provide permanent and freelance recruitment services.

IRSC
www.irsc.co.uk

> Specialising in temporary, permanent and secondment construction staff throughout the UK and world-wide.

JJP Recruitment
www.jjp.co.uk

> Specialist recruitment consultancy for professional staff within the construction industry, both permanent and freelance.

Select QS
www.selectqs.com

Select QS is a recruitment consultancy dedicated solely to the quantity surveying profession.

Education Jobs

Eteach.com
www.eteach.com

Eteach.com is a recruitment portal for education, providing unique services including teacher recruitment, discussion forums, advanced search facilities and resource guides. Teachers can register and use all the facilities on the site, including applying for jobs online, at no cost. There is also an NQT (Newly Qualified Teacher) zone specifically designed for those who are new to the teaching profession. It offers advice and useful information as well as a dependable support service for both student teachers and NQTs. Although there is no limit to the number of jobs you can apply for, the site has the following advice for teachers using the service: 'Be sure that your CV is regularly updated to ensure that potential employers are given the best possible impression'. Employers can also perform CV matches for their vacancies, which means that the job search becomes a two-way process, with jobs finding candidates. Unlike many other recruitment services, the site enables candidates to track the progress of their application, noting dates and interview arrangements as well as allowing them to keep in touch with the potential employer quickly and easily.

According to David Wilkes, a teacher from the West Midlands, the site is an invaluable resource for people seeking teaching jobs. 'I've just gained a post as the Head of English at a Primary School in Dudley as a direct result of searching on the site. It seems to be much easier to use than other similar sites and is certainly more up to date.'

Initial Education Personnel
www.iep.co.uk

Initial Education Personnel is an agency helping teachers find work in state primary and secondary schools in Greater London, Birmingham, Leeds and West Yorkshire.

Jobs in Education
www.jobsin.co.uk

> An online education recruitment database with a quick search facility and a CV submission service.

Mark Education Ltd
www.markltd.com

> A recruitment service boasting extensive knowledge of nursery, infant, junior, secondary and special needs education.

Masterlock
www.masterlock.co.uk

> Masterlock is an employment agency which operates in London and the South East.

NISS
www.niss.ac.uk

> This site links to the current vacancies pages of most major universities and colleges in the UK.

Time Plan
www.timeplan.com

> Time Plan enables candidates to search its job database, which comprises one of the largest selections of online teaching opportunities (permanent and temporary). After registering with the service, candidates can also add their details to a teacher database where they will be seen by schools throughout the UK and internationally.

Times Educational Supplement
www.jobs.tes.co.uk

> The *Times Educational Supplement's* job section, TES Jobs, refers to itself as 'the UK's number one site for teaching jobs'. Indeed, TES Jobs has more permanent UK teaching jobs than any other site, with new jobs posted every Friday. The free job service offers candidates an online application form (helping you to respond quickly to suitable advertisements), an e-mail alert option (to inform you of similar vacancies), local area information, school details from the TES Schools Directory and even a map to locate the school when you get the interview.

Graduate

Activate

www.activate.co.uk

> The Activate Web site includes a Career Search function which enables graduates to access a vast database of organisations which recruit graduates and undergraduates. Visitors can search by profession, UK area, organisation type, job type and expected qualifications.

Eurograduate

www.eurograduate.com

> An online database featuring thousands of graduate opportunities in Europe. You can search by country, industry, qualification or type of occupation.

Graduate Agency

www.graduate-agency.com

> A specialist free recruitment service for graduates. The Graduate Agency Web site advertises graduate opportunities on behalf of employers using both the Internet and local career services. Before applying for any vacancies listed on the site, visitors are required to complete an online primary application form.

Graduate Base

www.graduatebase.com

> Graduate Base is one of the leading graduate recruitment agencies.

Graduate Link

www.graduatelink.com

> Graduate Link is funded by the European Social Fund (ESF) and Yorkshire Humberside Universities Association (YHUA) and operates on behalf of the 13 university and higher education colleges in Yorkshire and Humberside to promote graduate recruitment in local companies. According to the Graduate Link Web site, the service 'was originally set up in response to the growing demand for graduates among small and medium sized companies. Since 1997 we have successfully filled vacancies for over 1,000 local employers.'

Graduate Recruitment
www.graduate-recruitment.co.uk

> Graduate Recruitment provides temporary and permanent work for graduates and has an online database of opportunities.

Graduate Recruitment Bureau
www.grb.uk.com

> The Graduate Recruitment Bureau is a recruitment agency not only for, but also run by, graduates. The service targets a number of companies for graduate job-seekers and defines a precise job specification based on the role, career progression, salary, benefits, travel, promotion prospects and future development. The sectors covered include IT, engineering, consultancy, retailing, PR, market research, media, publishing, finance, telecommunications, leisure, transport, manufacturing, recruitment, distribution and marketing. There are four ways for candidates to register. You can either e-mail your CV as a Word attachment, post your CV, pick up a FREEPOST registration card from your careers service, or complete the online registration form.

Milkround
www.milkround.co.uk

> Milkround is a jobs database aimed at new graduates. In addition to the database are a number of other services such as application advice, industry insights, up-to-date employment news and an online personality questionnaire. Users can sign up for e-mail alerts and receive personalised updates on relevant career news. They can also tailor their site experience by registering with the site. This means that each time they log on, Milkround highlights new opportunities that match the visitor's requirements. It is also possible to create and store covering letters and e-CVs at the site.

Prospects Web
www.prospects.csu.man.ac.uk

> The Prospects Web site provides hundreds of immediate vacancies for graduates as well as a database of graduate recruiters. Users of the service can focus on various employment categories including public sector, law, IT, science and engineering, finance and business, and teaching.

Reed Graduate Recruitment
www.reed.co.uk

>As the Reed site explains: 'One application to Reed Graduates makes your portfolio available to more than 2,500 professionally qualified consultants, based in over 280 branches across Ireland and the UK'. Candidates can also benefit from the Reed Graduates Direct service, which enables companies, selected by each candidate, to access portfolios directly. Graduates can register online using an electronic application form. Reed also offers a graduates' newsletter which helps candidates to keep up to date with all the latest opportunities.

IT and Web jobs

Burlingtons
www.burlingtons.co.uk

>Burlingtons is an IT agency specialising in mid-range and client service recruitment in the UK, Europe and US.

Computer Futures
www.computerfutures.co.uk

>An online computing magazine which enables candidates to search for vacancies and submit their CVs online.

Compuvac
www.compuvac.com

>Established in 1969, Compuvac provides a specialist IT recruitment service for the UK and Europe. It is now one of the UK's largest and most popular IT recruitment organisations.

Contracts 365
www.contracts365.co.uk

>A heavily promoted site specialising in IT contracts. As well as incorporating a database of agencies looking for contract staff the site also includes a 'Jobs by email' section.

Datum

www.datum.co.uk

> Although this is a general job search engine, the main emphasis is on IT jobs.

Dauphin Recruitment

www.dauphin.co.uk

> This London-based IT recruitment agency has an online search facility for contract and permanent vacancies.

Elan

www.elan.co.uk

> A frequent winner of *CMP* magazine's recruitment consultancy of the year award.

FTR

www.ftr.co.uk

> FTR is an IT recruitment consultancy which specialises in both contract and permanent posts throughout the UK and Europe. The company claims to be 'equally interested in the principles of ethical recruitment as [they] are in financial success'. This means, among other things, that they always get an applicant's consent prior to submitting them for any vacancy as well as accurately represent assignments to candidates to the best and fullest degree of their knowledge.

GCS Computer Recruitment

www.gcsltd.com

> GCS is a specialist UK IT recruitment consultancy with an online database and CV submission service. Candidates can also create a 'job-mail' profile to 'find all the current news and views in the world of IT recruitment'.

IT Moves

www.itmoves.com

> Another leading IT recruitment service.

IT Recruitment Network

www.itrnet.co.uk

> The IT Recruitment Network agency focuses on permanent jobs.

Laser Computer Recruitment

www.laserrec.co.uk

> Established in 1988, Laser now has a strong Web presence with a vast online database. Laser caters for experienced IT professionals in niche market areas such as e-commerce, CRM, PC networking and IT sales.

Paragon IT

www.paragon-it.com

> Paragon IT has a large pool of employers and candidates owing to its heavy investment in online and offline advertising. Candidates can choose to search contract jobs only, permanent jobs only, or both together.

Parity Resources

www.parityresources.co.uk

> Parity's client portfolio includes many of the FTSE 100 companies.

Plan Net

www.plan-net.co.uk

> Plan Net combines three divisions: the Support Division, the Consulting Division and the Recruitment Division.

Progressive Recruitment

www.progressive.co.uk

> Progressive Recruitment is one of the largest IT recruitment agencies in the UK. At the time we visited the site had over 4,000 current IT vacancies. Candidates can search by job type, keyword and region.

Recruit First

www.recruitfirst.com

> Recruit First is a solely Internet-based IT recruitment consultancy which uses an online process to 'facilitate the simplest and fastest solution to client recruitment needs and candidate aspirations'.

Sanderson Recruitment

www.sanderson-recruitment.co.uk

> Sanderson Recruitment specialises in computer and IT contract and permanent vacancies, including graduate vacancies.

Stepstone

www.stepstone.co.uk

> The Stepstone database includes a large IT section.

Marketing and sales jobs

ATA Group

www.ata.co.uk

> This recruitment company covers a broad range of technical and commercial sales disciplines from internal sales and field sales to sales management including industrial consumables, electrical products, service sector sales and fast-moving consumer goods. According to a statement on the ATA Web site: 'Candidates are interviewed by our consultants where rigorous procedures identify their relevant attributes. Personality profiling, career planning, product knowledge, market sector awareness, success and achievements, formal sales skills assessment, financial and emotional commitments and overall personal presentation are all evaluated.' The company operates from locations in Manchester, Leeds, Birmingham, Leicester, Bristol, Slough and Enfield.

CD Sales Recruitment

www.cdsalesrec.co.uk

> This recruitment company has six specialist divisions covering sales and marketing recruitment in specific industries: commercial, construction, technical, telecoms, IT and 'rec to rec' (recruitment to recruitment).

MAD

www.mad.co.uk

> MAD, the online community for marketing, media, advertising and design, has a vast job database which combines vacancy information from a wide variety of relevant trade publications.

Marketing Careerfile

www.marketing.haynet.com

> Marketing Careerfile is a service provided by *Marketing* magazine which is designed to help marketers find their next job quickly by providing valuable corporate and marketing focused information on the major recruiters of marketing staff. According to *Marketing* more than 10,000 readers/visitors have used the service to help them find their next job, and over 15,000 company briefings have been sent out since Careerfile's launch in November 1995. Ultimately, the Careerfile enables marketing job-seekers to become better briefed on companies from a wide range of market sectors.

On Target Recruitment

www.otrsales.co.uk

> An online database of UK sales jobs in the following sectors: building services, building products, business services, construction, electrical, electronics, finance, industrial, interiors, IT, lighting, mechanical engineering, office furniture and telecoms.

Retail

Harper Halsey Laroche

www.hhlrecruitment.co.uk

> Harper Halsey Laroche is an established 'Search and Selection' consultancy specialising in the retail and service sectors within the UK and internationally. The appointments are broken down into the following areas: retail management, buying and merchandising, human resources, operations, e-commerce and graduate appointments.

In Retail

www.inretail.co.uk

> A detailed recruitment site for the retail industry.

Retail Careers

www.retailcareers.co.uk

> Calling itself 'the UK's foremost web site dedicated to retail recruitment', Retail Careers features a vast selection of up-to-date vacancies from many of the UK's leading retailers and recruitment consultancies. Candidates can search by position (store management, e-commerce, graduate, etc.), salary and location.

Success Recruitment

www.successrecruit.co.uk

> One of the leading specialist retail recruitment consultancies in the UK. The company recruits within the following product sectors: fashion and clothing; homeware and interiors; jewellery and giftware; DIY and electricals, footwear and accessories; toys; stationery and hardgoods; and foods and convenience stores.

Talisman Retail

www.talismanretail.co.uk

> Talisman Retail specialises in recruitment in the retail, manufacturing, wholesale and e-commerce sectors in the UK and overseas. The company uses a mixture of personality profiling and aptitude testing.

Self-employment Resources

British Chambers of Commerce

www.britishchambers.org.uk

> The British Chambers of Commerce site provides a useful source of advice for small business owners. The site helps you locate your nearest chamber and details the advantages of joining the accredited network of businesses.

British Franchise Association
www.british-franchise.org.uk

> The British Franchise Association is a non-profit organisation representing franchised business.

Business Links
www.businesslinks.co.uk

> The Business Link Web site lists all the UK Business Links by county.

Inland Revenue
www.inlandrevenue.org.uk

> The online home of the Inland Revenue provides a guide to the tax considerations of starting your own business.

New Deal
www.newdeal.gov.uk

> This site details the government's schemes to help the unemployed back to work, including becoming self-employed and starting a business.

Prince's Trust
www.princes-trust.org

> If you are 18–25 and want to work for yourself but can't get the money you need to start your own business the Prince's Trust can offer a low interest loan of up to £5,000 and grants of up to £1,500 in special circumstances. It can also offer advice from a volunteer 'Business Mentor' during your first three years of trading.

Temporary work

Adecco
www.addecoalfredmarks.co.uk

> Recruitment company specialising in temporary vacancies.

Big Blue Dog
www.bigbluedog.com

The *Evening Standard*'s Big Blue Dog job finder service has an extensive temporary staff section.

Blue Arrow
www.bluearrow.co.uk

With a national network of over 200 branches and onsite service centres, Blue Arrow is one of the UK's largest recruitment companies. It handles a wide variety of temporary opportunities.

Brook Street
www.brookstreet.co.uk

Brook Street helps temporary work seekers by providing them with a Temporary Consultant, who talks them through the application process and asks questions about their personality, work experience and skills. To register for temporary work, site visitors simply need to complete an online registration form which is only two clicks away from the Brook Street home page.

Fish4Jobs
www.fish4jobs.co.uk

Temporary work for various industries is included on the Fish4Jobs Web site.

Manpower
www.manpower.co.uk

Nationwide recruitment agency which handles all types of work including temporary vacancies.

Office Angels
www.officeangels.co.uk

Office Angels is an office and secretarial recruitment agency with temporary and permanent vacancies. However, only a limited amount of temporary work information is available from the Office Angels Web site. For further information on any of the positions featured online, e-mail the branch featuring the vacancy of interest stating the job title and salary along with a copy of your CV.

Pertemps
www.pertemps.co.uk

> Pertemps is one of the leading temping agencies in the UK. The company is famed for its psychometric testing programmes for job applicants. Their GeneSys targeted personality profiling system provides an impressive range of occupational personality questionnaires and aptitude tests designed to profile temp candidates at all levels from shop floor to senior management positions. There are over 154 Pertemps branches throughout the UK.

Select
www.select.co.uk

> Select is one of the UK's leading commercial recruitment agencies placing more than 30,000 temporary staff each year, mainly in office-based roles such as secretarial, administrative, customer service, accounts and call centre jobs. Select operates 56 offices across the UK, recruiting temporary (and permanent) staff throughout the commercial sector.

Employer Directories

> Over the next few pages are listings of company Web sites relating to specific industries. Companies have been selected on the basis of their willingness to accept the Internet as an effective recruitment tool.

Accountancy

Baker Tilly
www.bakertilly.co.uk

> One of the leading UK accountancy firms with offices nationwide. Most jobs are in the business services area although there are also work opportunities in the tax department.

BDO Stoy Hayward
www.bdo.co.uk

> A large world-wide chartered accountancy firm specialising in auditing, tax consultancy and business recovery.

Grant Thornton
www.gt-recruitment.co.uk

> Grant Thornton has over 40 UK offices and hosts its own recruitment Web site.

HLB Kidsons
www.hlbkidsons.co.uk

> Business advisers and accountants based in London.

Mazars Neville Russell
www.mazars-nr.co.uk

> One of the largest chartered accountant firms in the UK.

Moore Stephens
www.moorestephens.co.uk

> Chartered accountants with 1,500 employees and offices nationwide.

The National Audit Office
www.open.gov.uk/nao/recruit/index.html

> The National Audit Office audits the accounts of all government departments and other public sector bodies such as the prison service and the Ministry of Defence.

Pornell Kerr Forster
www.pkf.co.uk

> A medium-sized firm which, according to its Web site, boasts a friendly working environment. Candidates must apply via an application form.

Architecture and construction

Balfour Beatty Construction
www.balfourbeattyconstruction.co.uk

> Departments include civil engineering, building and construction, and quantity surveying.

Building Design Partnership
www.bdp.co.uk

> With 900 employees Building Design Partnership is one of the largest architectural practices in the UK.

Foster and Partners
www.fosterandpartners.com

> Norman Foster's legendary practice attracts high-calibre architecture graduates.

Richard Rogers Partnership
www.rrp.co.uk

> Another internationally acclaimed architect firm.

Taylor Woodrow Construction
www.taywood.co.uk

> This Middlesex-based construction company has over 2,300 employees.

Broadcasting

BBC
www.bbc.co.uk/jobs

> The BBC's Web site provides a mine of information on vacancies within the company as well as general careers advice. It is justly referred to as one of the best company online recruitment services in the UK.

BskyB
www.sky.co.uk

> Sky keeps applications on file for three years and contacts applicants as and when suitable vacancies arise.

Capital Radio
www.capitalfm.com

> The London-based radio station offers useful career information on its Web site with an e-mail link to the personnel department.

Channel 4
www.channel4.com

> As speculative applications are not accepted and as no official graduate scheme is provided, administrative roles are generally considered the best way to get your foot in the Channel 4 door.

Channel 5
www.channel5.com

> Channel 5 vacancies are advertised in *The Guardian*'s media supplement which appears on Mondays.

Chrysalis
www.chrysalis.co.uk

> The Chrysalis group incorporates five sectors: TV, radio, music, media products and new media.

ITN
www.itn.co.uk

> Offers a graduate training scheme.

MTV
www.mtv.co.uk

> The world's most famous music television company.

Civil Service

Inland Revenue
www.inlandrevenue.gov.uk

> The public sector tax service provides a variety of job opportunities.

The Patent Office
www.patent.gov.uk

> The Patent Office administers the UK's intellectual property system.

Communications

British Telecom
www.bt.com/careers

> The BT site includes a very informative careers section.

Ericsson
www.ericsson.co.uk

> One of the world's largest telecommunications companies.

Motorola
www.motorola.com

> Motorola offers a wide variety of work opportunities including a two-year graduate training programme.

Nokia
www.nokia.co.uk/careers

> Nokia's careers section includes the latest vacancy information.

NTL
www.ntl.com

> At NTL all jobs incorporate a profit-related element based on company, division, department and individual achievement. This allows everyone to benefit from the success of the company.

One2One
www.one2one.co.uk

> The One2One Web site includes details of the latest job opportunities.

Orange
www.orange.co.uk

> Orange enables applicants to e-mail their CV to *jobs@orange.co.uk.*

Vodafone

www.vodafone.co.uk

> Vodafone's acquisition of Mannesman has made it Europe's largest company in terms of market capitalisation. The Vodafone Web site includes a graduate and careers section. Vodafone offers mentor-based graduate schemes in IT, engineering, marketing, human resources and finance.

Computing and new media

AOL

www.aol.co.uk

> AOL now incorporates Compuserve and Netscape Online. All positions are advertised internally. The AOL Web site also provides links to other Web sites with Internet-related job opportunities.

AltaVista

www.uk.altavista.com

> Candidates apply online to this search engine, portal and service provider.

Ask Jeeves

www.ask.co.uk

> According to its Web site the Ask Jeeves staff, known as 'Jeeviants', are very enthusiastic about the search engine they work for.

Dell

www.dell.com

> One of the largest computer systems companies in the world.

IBM

www.ibm.com/employment

> IBM includes an employer application form on its Web site.

Microsoft
www.microsoft.com/uk/jobs

> Microsoft UK's job section includes comprehensive vacancy details for Microsoft and MSN.co.uk.

Oracle
www.uk.oracle.com

> Oracle's job applications take place exclusively via the Web.

Financial services

> As well as visiting the company web sites listed below, job hunters interested in the finance and banking industry should take a look at **Jobs in the Money** (*www.jobsinthemoney.com*), a recruitment site for financial professionals.

Abbey National
www.abbeynational.plc.uk/recruitment

> The Abbey National Web site's recruitment section enables candidates to apply online.

Barclays
www.barclays.com
www.graduatecareers.barclays.com

> Barclays has set up a separate site in its bid to recruit high-calibre graduates. Online application is available for graduate positions.

Deutsche Bank
www.db.com

> One of the world's biggest global investment banks with 500 annual graduate vacancies in the UK.

Halifax
www.halifaxplc.com

> The former building society which became a bank in 1997 offers a variety of job opportunities within Halifax Direct, Halifax Life and Halifax Property Services.

HSBC
www.hsbc.com/recruitment

> HSBC.com's recruitment section provides relevant vacancy and career information.

J P Morgan
www.jpmorgan.com/careers

> An investment banking company with a useful careers sections and online application procedure.

Lloyds TSB
www.lloydstsb.co.uk
www.lloydstsbgraduate.co.uk

> Similar to Barclays, Lloyds TSB provide a graduate recruitment Web site allowing candidates to apply online.

Merrill Lynch
www.ml.com/careers

> The global financial management and advisory company uses psychometric tests in its recruitment process.

Natwest
www.natwest.co.uk

> One of the UK's largest banks offering jobs in retail banking, corporate banking, mortgage services, insurance and card services.

Schroders
www.schroders.com

> The institutional asset management company encourages online applications.

The Royal Bank of Scotland
www.rbs.co.uk

> Scotland's largest financial and banking employer.

Insurance

AXA Sun Life
www.sunlife.co.uk
> A Bristol-based company with offices nationwide.

Cornhill Insurance
www.cornhill.co.uk
> Recruitment information is included on the Cornhill Web site.

Direct Line
www.directline.com
> The Direct Line Web site lists all the regional office addresses.

Law

Clifford Chance
www.cliffordchance.com
> Leading commercial law firm based in London.

Norton Rose
www.nortonrose.com
> An international city law firm with worldwide offices.

Simmons and Simmons
www.simmons-simmons.com
> International law firm with lots of overseas opportunities.

Leisure and travel

British Airways
www.britishairways.com
> British Airways offer a variety of work opportunities.

Forte Hotels
www.forte-hotels.com
> The Forte Web site includes vacancy information.

JD Wetherspoon plc
www.jdwetherspoon.co.uk

> Winner of the Pub Company of the Year award in 2000.

Marketing

> There are a number of online recruitment agencies specialising in marketing, advertising and PR jobs. Sites such as **Major Players** (*www.majorplayers.co.uk*) and **Source That Job** (*www.sourcethatjob.com*) provide information on vacancies as well as services designed to matchmake candidates with the right job.
>
> However, as these agencies do not cover every marketing and media-related job out there job seekers interested in working in these industries should also visit company Web sites for vacancy information.
>
> Outlined below are some of the advertising and marketing companies which use the web to recruit new employees.

Advertising agencies

Abbot Mead Vickers BBDO Ltd
www.amvbddo.co.uk

> Abbot Mead Vickers BBDO Ltd is the largest advertising agency in the UK and has a workforce of over 300.

Bartle Bogle Hegarty
www.bbh.co.uk

> Another global agency.

Euro RSCG Wnek Gosper Ltd
www.eurorscg.co.uk

> Set up in 1994, Euro RSCG is a London-based consultancy which has clients such as Cadbury, Evian and Peugeot. Candidates are expected to apply via the employer application form only.

J Walter Thompson

www.jwt.com

> One of the biggest UK agencies with offices world-wide. Applications are made via CV and covering letter.

Leo Burnett Ltd

www.leoburnett.com

> A global agency with offices in London. Offers graduate training for account management and planners.

Lowe Howard-Spink Ltd

www.lowehoward-spink.co.uk

> Another large London-based advertising agency.

M & C Saatchi

www.mcsaatchi.com

> One of the world's newest but most well-respected advertising agencies.

Ogilvy and Mather

www.ogilvy.com

> Excellent positions available.

Saatchi and Saatchi

www.saatchi-saatchi.com

> Calling itself an 'ideas communication' company Saatchi and Saatchi offers account management and media planning roles.

Marketing and PR agencies

Burson Marsteller

www.bm.com

> A leading London-based PR firm which enables candidates to submit CVs via their Web site.

Charles Baker BSHG Worldwide

www.cbaker.co.uk

> A PR and marketing agency specialising in youth marketing, healthcare, travel, leisure and public affairs.

Grayling
www.graylinggroup.com

> Grayling is a PR and marketing agency with offices in London, Bristol, Birmingham, Leeds, Cardiff and Glasgow.

Hill and Knowlton
www.hillandknowlton.co.uk

> Another London-based PR agency offering a year-long graduate training scheme starting every September.

Shandwick
www.shandwick.com

> Shandwick PR agency has 15 offices throughout the UK.

Professional services

Arthur Andersen
www.arthurandersen.com

> Arthur Andersen offers a range of business and financial services to clients all over the world. It has over 650 graduate vacancies annually.

Ernst and Young
www.eyuk.com

> Provides a variety of services ranging from audit and assistance to management consultancy.

KPMG
www.kpmgcareers.co.uk

> Professional service firm with its own careers Web site.

PriceWaterhouse Coopers
www.pwcglobal.com/uk

> PriceWaterhouse Coopers is the largest professional services organisation in the world employing over 150,000 people in more than 150 countries. The UK firm has 30 offices nationwide.

Retail

Arcadia
www.arcadiagroup.co.uk

> The Arcadia group consists of 13 fashion brands including Dorothy Perkins, Evans, Top Shop and Warehouse. Encourages online applications for management and marketing positions.

Boots
www.bootscareers.co.uk

> Boots has its own separate career Web site where candidates can apply online.

Debenhams
www.debenhams.com

> Debenhams offers a wide range of job opportunities at all levels.

Iceland
www.iceland.co.uk

> The Iceland Web site includes recruitment information.

L'Oréal
www.loreal.com

> As one of the world's leading retail brands, L'Oréal offers a wide variety of marketing products.

Marks and Spencer
www.marks-and-spencer.com

> Marks and Spencer offers candidates the choice of online and offline application methods. Any job enquiries can be sent to *recruit@marks-and-spencer.com*.

Procter and Gamble
www.pg.com

> Job enquiries and applications should be sent to *recunitedkingdom@pg.com*.

Tesco

www.tesco.co.uk

> Tesco is now one of the UK's leading food retailers as well as the world's most successful online grocer. As such it takes its recruitment process very seriously.

Unilever

www.unilever.com
www.ucmds.com

> Unilever has its own graduate recruitment Web site.

Glossary

address book A directory in a Web browser where you can store and manage e-mail addresses. Address books are particularly useful for online job-seekers who may be in contact with various employers, recruitment sites and career advisors.

ADSL Asymmetric Digital Subscriber Line: a high-speed, high-bandwidth telephone line which helps your computer to download Web sites and e-mail messages faster.

AGCAS The Association of Graduate Careers Advisory Services.

anti-sites Anti-sites are Web sites which are devoted to criticising a company or organisation. Usually, they are set up by an aggrieved employee who has been unable to contribute their opinion to the company's Web site. Anti-sites are often intended to parody or replicate the site they are targeting. In some instances, an anti-site can beat the official site in the search engine rankings by generating more site visits. They can be useful for job-hunters wanting to find out inside information on a company they may have previously considered working for.

article The name given to a single message posted to a discussion group.

assessment centre An assessment centre is a place where recruiting employers can analyse the skills of candidates through team work, psychometric tests, personality questionnaires and other methods.

attachment A file added to an e-mail to be sent via the e-mail system. E-CVs are normally sent as attachments.

backlink checking A means of finding out which Web pages are linked to a specific Web site. Many search engines enable users to conduct 'backlink searches' by entering the name of a Web site into the search box preceded by a special command (such as 'link'). AltaVista and HotBot are two of the most popular search engines to offer this facility. The backlink checking process can be automated by using a service such as LinkPopularity.com, which enables users to search for linking sites at various search engines at once. Backlink checking can help job-seekers find useful information on a company which they might not have otherwise come across.

binaries Files attached to discussion group articles. You may have cause to post your CV as a binary file.

bookmark A bookmark is a tool available on most Web browsers which enables you to store useful web addresses.

Boolean search A search following the inclusion or exclusion of Web sites containing certain words through the use of Boolean operators such as AND, NOT and OR.

brochureware A derogatory term used to describe commercial Web content which resembles a company brochure. Brochureware sites tend to be of little use for the job-seeker as they are usually full of biased information.

browser Software that allows you to access the Internet and World Wide Web. Internet Explorer and Netscape Navigator are the most commonly-used browsers.

cancel option Useful in e-mail and discussion group systems as it allows you to delete a message before or just after posting an e-mail message or newsgroup article.

candidate database An online database consisting of job seekers' CV details. Candidate databases are usually found on recruitment sites.

click through The term 'click through' is used to describe the action which occurs when a user clicks onto any hyperlink.

community A group of Internet users with a shared interest or concept who interact with each other in newsgroups, mailing-list discussion groups and other online interactive forums. There are many job-seeking and employment-based communities.

cookie A cookie is a small file that is stored on a user's computer when commanded to do so by software at a Web site. Web sites use cookies to monitor and recognise users who visit them. When a user returns to the Web site, the relevant Web server can read its cookie and structure its Web pages accordingly. Although cookies are popular among online recruitment sites, many users view them as a security or privacy hazard.

covering e-mail An e-mail message sent with an e-CV to employers.

crawler A type of search engine 'robot'.

cross-posting The act of posting the same message into several different news or discussion groups simultaneously.

cyberspace Term originally coined in the sci-fi novels of William Burroughs, referring to the online world and its communication networks.

database site This is the fastest growing type of recruitment site. Typically, job-seekers are asked to complete an extensive online form that builds a profile of their skills. This is then matched against the employers' requirements.

discussion groups Discussion groups are online discussion areas centred around a subject of common interest. People post message to the groups which all the other members can read.

disintermediation A term used to refer to the Internet's ability to cut out intermediaries or 'middlemen'. The Internet enables companies to communicate with job-hunters directly, bypassing intermediaries such as recruitment agencies and newspaper job supplements.

domain name An officially registered Web site address of a site.

dot.com Used to refer to a company based exclusively online.

download The term used to describe the transfer of a computer file from the Internet to a PC.

drownloading The act of simultaneously downloading so many files that a computer crashes.

e-CV Electronic CV: a CV document sent via e-mail either as an attachment or appended to the end of an e-mail message.

e-mail Electronic mail: a message sent across the Internet, or the act of transferring messages between computers, mobile phones or other enabled devices. E-mail can be used by job-seekers to conduct primary research as well as to send their application details to employers.

e-mail services Many recruitment sites offer e-mail services which enables job-seekers to receive vacancy and industry news tailored to their specifications.

e-mail system The collective e-mail software system which allows you to create, send, receive e-mail messages.

employment auctions Employment auctions enable individuals to submit personal profiles to the Web, together with ideal assignments and fees, and interested companies then bid on those they want to hire.

encryption The conversion of information into a code so that people will be unable to read it without a secret password. Encryption technology is of particular importance for recruitment sites which need to protect user information such as CV details.

e-TV Interactive television, accessed via a computer or a TV set.

e-zines Online interactive magazines which only exist on the Internet.

flame A hostile or aggressive message sent via e-mail or posted into an online newsgroup. Typically, flame messages are sent in response to spam or unsolicited commercial e-mail. If a flame message is responded to in a similarly hostile manner, it can lead to a 'flame war'.

forums Newsgroups, mailing list discussion groups, chat rooms and other online areas which allow you to read, post and respond to messages.

freeware Free software programs.

gateway sites Gateway sites are Web sites which have compiled and organised a large amount of Web-based information around a certain topic, such as recruitment. Many search engine sites in effect act as gateways. For instance, Yahoo! UK's employment section acts as a useful gateway for Internet job-seekers.

history list A record of visited Web pages you can access through your browser. It can help you find useful sites you haven't been able to bookmark.

hit A hit is a transfer from a Web server to a Web browser. Every time an Internet user clicks onto a Web page he or she is causing at least one transfer. If a text page has no images it counts as one hit. If the page also incorporates an image file, it causes two hits. As most Web pages have at least one image file (usually they have more) it is inaccurate to equate the number of hits with the number of visitors although many recruitment sites apparently do so.

home page The first and/or main page on a Web site.

HTML Hypertext Mark-up Language: a computer code used to build and develop Web pages.

hyperlink Most commonly found on Web pages, hyperlinks are either images or pieces of text which, when a user clicks on them, lead to other Web pages. They can be used to connect *internally*, to connect Web pages within the same site, as well as *externally*, to link to other Web sites. They can also be used in e-mail messages, for example to include the address of a company's Web site. This is especially useful when sending e-CVs as it means applicants can provide links to Web sites of companies they have worked for and any academic institutions they have attended. Also referred to as a hypertext link.

hyper time A term used to convey the apparent fast pace and decentralised nature of Internet time.

index The searchable catalogue of documents created by search engine software.

information overload The situation of having found so much information on the Web that your job-seeking efforts are being hindered.

Internet The Internet includes Web sites, e-mail, newsgroups and other forums. This is a public network, though many of the computers connected to it are also part of *Intranets*. It uses the Internet Protocol (IP) as a communication standard.

ISP Internet Service Provider: a firm that provides Internet services such as e-mail and Web access.

keywords Words used by search engines to help find Web sites.

keyword search A search for documents containing one or more words that are specified by a search engine user.

links Text or graphic icons that move you to different Web pages or sites. Links are activated by clicking them with a mouse.

log on/off To access/leave the Internet.

lurk The act of visiting an Internet news or discussion group without taking part. Lurking is important because inappropriate messages are likely to receive a hostile response from newsgroup members, and may even be considered as 'spam'. Lurking in relevant newsgroups can also be an effective means of searching for job vacancy information.

mailing list A collection of e-mail addresses.

mail server A remote computer (usually your ISP) enabling you to send and receive e-mails.

meta-tags The keyword and description commands in a Web page's code used to help search engines index the relevant Web site.

moderator A person in charge of a newsgroup, mailing list discussion group or similar forum. A moderator edits any unwelcome messages.

net Shorthand for Internet.

net-head Internet obsessed individual.

netiquette The etiquette of the Internet, particularly e-mail.

news reader Software enabling you to search, read, post and arrange newsgroup messages.

offline Used to denote any activity or situation which does not involve being connected to the Internet.

online The state of being connected to the Internet.

online application form An application form which can be filled in at a company Web site. Marks and Spencer (*www.marks-and-spencer.co.uk)* and *Dyson (www.dyson.com)* are two companies which use online application forms as part of their recruitment process.

phrase search A search for documents containing an exact sentence or phrase specified by a search engine user.

POP Post Office Protocol – the most common Internet standard for e-mail. Once POP is in use, all new incoming messages are downloaded from the server as soon as the e-mail account is accessed. All POP e-mails are stored on the server until the user removes them.

psychometric tests Assessment tests used by employers and recruiters to gauge the personality and psychological profile of applicants.

real world Everything outside the Internet.

recruitment sites Recruitment sites are either recruitment agencies or job posting sites which provide vacancy information for job-seekers. Very often these sites also include general careers advice and newsworthy information on specific industries.

refresh The act of reloading a Web site page or site.

robot A software tool used by search engines to find and examine Web sites.

salary calculator Salary calculators are online tools used at recruitment sites (such as *Reed.co.uk*) which can help people work out what they could be earning elsewhere in the country.

search engine A site which enables you to conduct a keyword search of indexed information on its database.

self-assessment tests Self-assessment tests in this context range from personality and psychometric tests to assessments of your current career status. There are various Web sites enabling you to conduct self-assessment tests online.

shell forms Another name for a Web-based application form.

signature (file) Information added to the end of an e-mail message that identifies the sender's details.

snail mail The 'real-world' postal service.

spam Unsolicited bulk e-mail, usually sent for commercial purposes. Spam is used by some recruitment companies as a cheap form of advertising, although is generally considered offensive and unwelcome by the Internet community. Spamming is considered unethical because the cost is paid by the recipient's site or server, not the sender's. Various Internet bodies, such as the Coalition Against Unsolicited E-mail (CAUCE), campaign actively against spam and those individuals or organisations accused of spamming. The term originates from the Monty Python sketch in which customers at a 'greasy spoon' café are served spam with everything regardless of whether it was part of their order.

spam CVs E-CVs sent by recruitment agencies to employers without their permission.

spider A type of search engine 'robot'.

SSL Secure Sockets Layer: the main type of secure server used to transfer sensitive information. SSL technology is used by recruitment sites in order to protect personal information provided by job-seekers.

stemming The ability for a search to include the 'stem' of words.

synchronous communication Interaction between Internet users occurring in 'real time'.

top level domain The concluding part of a domain name, such as the .com or .co.uk suffixes.

URL Uniform Resource Locator: a full Web address, for example: *http://www.jobsite.co.uk.*

vacancy database An online database consisting of job vacancy details posted by employers. Vacancy databases are usually found on recruitment sites.

WAP Wireless Application Protocol: a technology which enables people to access the Internet via mobile phones and other mobile devices.

Web master Someone in charge of a Web site.

Web page A single document stored at a Web site.

Web site A collection of Web pages which can be accessed via the same URL (see above).

World Wide Web The World Wide Web software system running across the Internet consists of (literally) billions of Web pages, usually containing text, images and HTML links.

Further Reading

The Circle of Innovation, Tom Peters (Coronet)

Finding a Job on the Internet, Brendan Murphy (Internet Handbooks)

Job Hunt on the Net, Julie-Ann Amos (How To Books)

Job Hunting for Dummies, Max Messmer (IDG)

Job Hunting Made Easy, John Branham and David Cox (Kogan Page)

Net That Job!, Irene Krechowiecka (Kogan Page)

Surfing Your Career, Hilary Nickell (How to Books)

What Color Is Your Parachute?, Richard Nelson Bolles (TenSpeed Press)

Index

The Job Application Handbook
Sell yourself to an employer using proven strategies and effective techniques

Judith Johnstone

Whether you're leaving college, re-entering the job market, facing redundancy or wanting to change your existing job, you need to equip yourself with good job hunting skills. This handbook reveals the best ways to approach potential employers. Use the checklists, techniques and samples throughout to assess your skills, plan your strategy, and produce focused CVs, winning letters and application forms. Includes job searching on the Internet.

160 pages 1 85703 636 0. 5th edition.

Job Hunt on the Net
Self-marketing techniques to help you search for vacancies and apply for jobs online

Julie-Ann Amos

'. . . .will give you a far better chance of finding a job than just traditional means.' *The Guardian.*

61 pages 1 85703 637 9.

Surfing Your Career
1000 specialist web sites. Career opportunities. Job hunting and training

Hilary Nickell

The first comprehensive and professionally evaluated guide to careers information on the Net. 'Even an experienced surfer needs help when looking for career information on the Internet. Hilary Nickell is just the bloke to give it...an excellent and comprehensive guide.' *What PC.* '...compiled for both job changers and those considering career change for the first time...its breadth and ease of use are its strengths.' *Phoenix: Careers Service Journal.*

176 pages 1 85703 586 0.

Using the Internet
How to get started and find what you want for business, education and pleasure

Graham Jones

'A comprehensive guide for the novice.' *Computeractive.*
'Practical, down-to-earth advice.' *Focus on Business Education.*

128 pages 1 85703 504 6. 3rd edition

Handling Tough Job Interviews
Perform well in interviews whatever the circumstances

Julie-Ann Amos

This book covers various types of interview, from recruitment agencies and head-hunters, through to interviews with employers and Human Resources departments. HR consultant Julie-Ann Amos guides you through the whole recruitment process and provides useful advice on handling interviews with senior management, dealing with psychometrics and assessment centres, and discussing and agreeing a job offer.

144 pages 1 85703 720 0.

Taking Control of Your Own Career
Using NLP and other techniques to get the working life you want

Barbara Buffton

'Important careers issues are covered along with a range of appropriate techniques for handling them.' *Nick Evans, Occupational Psychologist, Newscheck.* 'Discover how to decide what you really want to do and motivate yourself.' *London Evening Standard.*

144 pages 1 85703 395 7.

Passing That Interview
Your step-by-step guide to coming out on top
Judith Johnstone

Using a systematic and practical approach, this book takes you step-by-step through the essential pre-interview groundwork, the interview itself, and what you can learn from the experience. It contains sample pre- and post-interview correspondence, together with a guide to further reading, and useful contact addresses. 'A fresh approach to a well-documented subject.' *Newscheck, Careers Service Bulletin.* 'A complete step-by-step guide.' *The Association of Business Executives.*

144 pages 1 85703 538 0. 5th edition.

Getting Your First Job
How to get the job that will give you the right start
Penny Hitchin

This practical guide shows you how to overcome the particular challenges of getting your first job. 'A comprehensive guide to jobhunting.' *Phoenix – Association of Careers Advisory Services.*

126 pages 1 85703 549 6. 2nd edition.

Getting Started on the Internet

Irene Krechowiecka

- *Access a world of information*
- *Master email and newsgroups*

'All you'll need for only a fiver.' *Computer Active.* 'an excellent small book... clear instructions, lots of advice and warnings to help you safeguard your computer from viruses, keep safe and keep costs down... can you afford not to have it? *Focus on Business Education.*

83 pages 1 85703 516 X

1000 Best Websites

- *Access the most useful site around*
- *Avoid hours of fruitless searching*
- *Link to an associated web site*

Bruce Durie

Art, Business, Computers, Education, Entertainment, Finance, Friends, Games, Health, Home, Kids, News, Nutrition, Pets, Science, Shopping, Sports, Travel, Writing and more... This popular family reference includes a useful glossary and index, together with searching tips. '... comprehensive and easy to use.' *The Bookseller.* Bruce Durie divides his time between writing and consultancy, and is the author of several How To books.

216 pages 1 85703 657 3

Enhancing Your Employability
How to make sure you achieve a fulfilling and rewarding career

Roderic Ashley

'Practical advice on improving your prospects.' *The Guardian.*
'of great benefit to people not only searching for improvement
and satisfaction in their chosen career, but also those seeking to
find balance and perspective in their lives.' *Executive PA.*

144 pages 1 85703 371 X

Writing a CV That Works
How to develop and use your key marketing tool

Paul McGee

This popular book shows you how to unlock the potential of
your most powerful marketing tool, whatever your background
or current situation. 'This book certainly gave me the initiative
to go for it!... out of the three jobs that my reformed CV was
sent to I received three interviews. I am now looking forward
to starting my new job at the beginning of the month.' *A
reader from London.*

128 pages 1 85703 365 5 2nd edition